What you track grows.

We created this special journal to help you organize your intention towards building your network marketing business.

For just 60 minutes a day within a 90 day cycle, this tool can help you build strong daily habits.

XX

D1501180

Haley, Sandy & Wade

Please use hashtag #newhabits90 and tag @90dayhabitsjournal on your social media stories/posts when using this journal. Be sure to also check out our website for updates and exclusive offers. www.90dayhabitsjournal.com

We appreciate word of mouth advertising/shoutouts/tags & swipe up call to actions on social media! Thank you, thank you, thank you

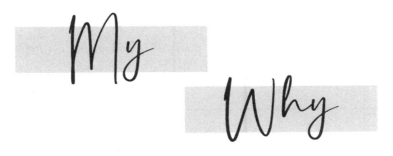

Do you know your WHY?

The purpose, cause or beliefs that inspire you to do what you do?

An integral part of starting any business is knowing WHY you are doing it. Your WHY will be a driving force in your journey and something that will keep you going when you meet obstacles. When your WHY is big enough, obstacles cease to exist. Your WHY will also show others the power behind your decision to build a business and where you are headed. Working hard for something we do not care about is called stress, working hard for something we love is called passion. Construct a clear and concise WHY and build a strong foundation for your business.

Concisely answer the below questions and then thread it together for your why statement.

1. WHY are you deciding to build this business? (Peel back the layers to get your real WHY)

_____

_____

_____

_____

_____

2. Why is this so important to you? Get very specific here. How do you see this changing your life, affecting your family, impacting the lives of others, helping you build a legacy and get where you want to be long-term?

_____

_____

_____

_____

_____

3. If you DON'T achieve your WHY, what is the pain you will experience? What cost will you have paid in your life by NOT taking action to build this business?

_____

_____

_____

_____

_____

4. Envision your life five years into the future. If you don't achieve your WHY, where will you be and what will you have given up? Who or what was not worth it to you to follow through with your WHY?

_____

_____

_____

_____

_____

5. Now think where you will be in 5 years into the future if you did achieve your WHY. How would you have grown, what would you have contributed to the world, or your family, how would you feel achieving your life goals, what would you experience, how would it affect your confidence?

_____

_____

_____

_____

_____

Bonus I: Share your WHY with your mentors and tell them they have permission to revisit your WHY with you when times get tough

Bonus II: Share your WHY on video on your social media account(s)

Vision Casting

"The future belongs to those who believe in the beauty of their dreams" - Eleanor Roosevelt

If you keep doing what you are doing...where will you be in 5 years? A lot can change in a short amount of time with FOCUS. Close your eyes for a moment while intentionally taking deep breaths and imagine if there were **no limits** to what you could do, be, have, buy, places you could go, and beyond, what would you create? If you knew you could not fail...what do you truly desire?

Family | Relationships | Health | Travel | Spiritual | Finances | Career | Giving Back | Personal Growth | Lifestyle

1.	26.
2.	27.
3.	28.
4.	29.
5.	30.
6.	31.
7.	32.
8.	33.
9.	34.
10.	35.
11.	36.
12.	37.
13.	38.
14.	39.
15.	40.
16.	41.
17.	42.
18.	43.
19.	44.
20.	45.
21.	46.
22.	47.
23.	48.
24.	49.
25.	50.

100
Person List

	Host	1-on-1	Samples	Live Event	3 Way Call	Recorded Video
1.	☐	☐	☐	☐	☐	☐
2.	☐	☐	☐	☐	☐	☐
3.	☐	☐	☐	☐	☐	☐
4.	☐	☐	☐	☐	☐	☐
5.	☐	☐	☐	☐	☐	☐
6.	☐	☐	☐	☐	☐	☐
7.	☐	☐	☐	☐	☐	☐
8.	☐	☐	☐	☐	☐	☐
9.	☐	☐	☐	☐	☐	☐
10.	☐	☐	☐	☐	☐	☐
11.	☐	☐	☐	☐	☐	☐
12.	☐	☐	☐	☐	☐	☐
13.	☐	☐	☐	☐	☐	☐
14.	☐	☐	☐	☐	☐	☐
15.	☐	☐	☐	☐	☐	☐
16.	☐	☐	☐	☐	☐	☐
17.	☐	☐	☐	☐	☐	☐
18.	☐	☐	☐	☐	☐	☐
19.	☐	☐	☐	☐	☐	☐
20.	☐	☐	☐	☐	☐	☐
21.	☐	☐	☐	☐	☐	☐
22.	☐	☐	☐	☐	☐	☐
23.	☐	☐	☐	☐	☐	☐
24.	☐	☐	☐	☐	☐	☐
25.	☐	☐	☐	☐	☐	☐

100

Person List

	Host	1-on-1	Samples	Live Event	3 Way Call	Recorded Video
26.	☐	☐	☐	☐	☐	☐
27.	☐	☐	☐	☐	☐	☐
28.	☐	☐	☐	☐	☐	☐
29.	☐	☐	☐	☐	☐	☐
30.	☐	☐	☐	☐	☐	☐
31.	☐	☐	☐	☐	☐	☐
32.	☐	☐	☐	☐	☐	☐
33.	☐	☐	☐	☐	☐	☐
34.	☐	☐	☐	☐	☐	☐
35.	☐	☐	☐	☐	☐	☐
36.	☐	☐	☐	☐	☐	☐
37.	☐	☐	☐	☐	☐	☐
38.	☐	☐	☐	☐	☐	☐
39.	☐	☐	☐	☐	☐	☐
40.	☐	☐	☐	☐	☐	☐
41.	☐	☐	☐	☐	☐	☐
42.	☐	☐	☐	☐	☐	☐
43.	☐	☐	☐	☐	☐	☐
44.	☐	☐	☐	☐	☐	☐
45.	☐	☐	☐	☐	☐	☐
46.	☐	☐	☐	☐	☐	☐
47.	☐	☐	☐	☐	☐	☐
48.	☐	☐	☐	☐	☐	☐
49.	☐	☐	☐	☐	☐	☐
50.	☐	☐	☐	☐	☐	☐

100 *Person List*

	Host	1-on-1	Samples	Live Event	3 Way Call	Recorded Video
51.	☐	☐	☐	☐	☐	☐
52.	☐	☐	☐	☐	☐	☐
53.	☐	☐	☐	☐	☐	☐
54.	☐	☐	☐	☐	☐	☐
55.	☐	☐	☐	☐	☐	☐
56.	☐	☐	☐	☐	☐	☐
57.	☐	☐	☐	☐	☐	☐
58.	☐	☐	☐	☐	☐	☐
59.	☐	☐	☐	☐	☐	☐
60.	☐	☐	☐	☐	☐	☐
61.	☐	☐	☐	☐	☐	☐
62.	☐	☐	☐	☐	☐	☐
63.	☐	☐	☐	☐	☐	☐
64.	☐	☐	☐	☐	☐	☐
65.	☐	☐	☐	☐	☐	☐
66.	☐	☐	☐	☐	☐	☐
67.	☐	☐	☐	☐	☐	☐
68.	☐	☐	☐	☐	☐	☐
69.	☐	☐	☐	☐	☐	☐
70.	☐	☐	☐	☐	☐	☐
71.	☐	☐	☐	☐	☐	☐
72.	☐	☐	☐	☐	☐	☐
73.	☐	☐	☐	☐	☐	☐
74.	☐	☐	☐	☐	☐	☐
75.	☐	☐	☐	☐	☐	☐

100

Person List

	Host	1-on-1	Samples	Live Event	3 Way Call	Recorded Video
76.	☐	☐	☐	☐	☐	☐
77.	☐	☐	☐	☐	☐	☐
78.	☐	☐	☐	☐	☐	☐
79.	☐	☐	☐	☐	☐	☐
80.	☐	☐	☐	☐	☐	☐
81.	☐	☐	☐	☐	☐	☐
82.	☐	☐	☐	☐	☐	☐
83.	☐	☐	☐	☐	☐	☐
84.	☐	☐	☐	☐	☐	☐
85.	☐	☐	☐	☐	☐	☐
86.	☐	☐	☐	☐	☐	☐
87.	☐	☐	☐	☐	☐	☐
88.	☐	☐	☐	☐	☐	☐
89.	☐	☐	☐	☐	☐	☐
90.	☐	☐	☐	☐	☐	☐
91.	☐	☐	☐	☐	☐	☐
92.	☐	☐	☐	☐	☐	☐
93.	☐	☐	☐	☐	☐	☐
94.	☐	☐	☐	☐	☐	☐
95.	☐	☐	☐	☐	☐	☐
96.	☐	☐	☐	☐	☐	☐
97.	☐	☐	☐	☐	☐	☐
98.	☐	☐	☐	☐	☐	☐
99.	☐	☐	☐	☐	☐	☐
100.	☐	☐	☐	☐	☐	☐

Monthly Overview

MONTH

This Month's Goals :

Non-Negotiables :

Stretch Goals :

Important Action Steps/ Events

○ _____
○ _____
○ _____
○ _____
○ _____
○ _____
○ _____
○ _____
○ _____
○ _____

SU	M	TU	W	TH	F	SA

Notes

"The reason most people never reach their goals is that they don't define them, or ever seriously consider them as believable or achievable. Winners can tell where they are going, what they plan to do along the way, and whp will be sharing the adventure with them."
- Denis Waitley

30 Conversations
in 30 Days

Write down the names of each NEW person you present your product/service to.
This can be in person, a 1-on-1 meeting, at an event or online (including recorded presentations).
Your goal is at least 30 conversations per month. How close are you?

_____

_____

_____

_____

_____

_____

_____

_____

_____

_____

_____

_____

_____

_____

_____

_____

_____

_____

_____

_____

_____

_____

_____

_____

_____

_____

_____

_____

_____

_____

What You Track Grows ...
So Lets Start Tracking

Date: 05·27·2021

60 Minutes of Daily Focus

20 Minutes ~ Mindset
Gratitude: Today I'm **Grateful** For..

gracias a Dios por un dia mas de vida
y Porque mi niño esta mucho mejor.

- ☑ Gratitude - 1 Minute
- ☐ Meditation - 2 Minutes
- ☐ Affirmations - 2 Minutes

- ☐ Movement - 5 Minutes
- ☐ Read - 10 Minutes

Today's 3 Non Negotiables:

_____
_____
_____

To Do:

1. _____ ☐
2. _____ ☐
3. _____ ☐

4. _____ ☐
5. _____ ☐
6. _____ ☐

| Done ☑ | Extend ☑ | Delegate ◎ | Remove ☒ |

20 Minutes ~ Relationship Building
People you introduce your product/service to, new connections and reconnections.

Name	Method of Follow Up/Notes
1. _____	_____
2. _____	_____
3. _____	_____
4. _____	_____
5. _____	_____

20 Minutes ~ Follow Up
Prospects, Clients and Team

Name	Method of Follow Up/Notes
1. _____	_____
2. _____	_____
3. _____	_____
4. _____	_____
5. _____	_____

☐ Instagram
☐ Facebook

☐ Birthday Acknowledgement
☐ Recorded Training Audio/Video

Win(s) For The Day:

_____

_____

_____

You are one of a kind.

What You Track Grows ...
So Lets Start Tracking

Date: _____

60 Minutes of Daily Focus

20 Minutes ~ Mindset
Gratitude: Today I'm **Grateful** For..

_____

_____

_____

_____

_____

☐ Gratitude - 1 Minute   ☐ Movement - 5 Minutes

☐ Meditation - 2 Minutes   ☐ Read - 10 Minutes

☐ Affirmations - 2 Minutes

Today's 3 Non Negotiables:

_____

_____

_____

To Do:

1. _____ ☐   4. _____ ☐

2. _____ ☐   5. _____ ☐

3. _____ ☐   6. _____ ☐

| Done ☑ | Extend ☑ | Delegate ⊡ | Remove ☒ |

20 Minutes ~ Relationship Building
People you introduce your product/service to, new connections and reconnections.

Name	Method of Follow Up/Notes
1. _____	_____
2. _____	_____
3. _____	_____
4. _____	_____
5. _____	_____

20 Minutes ~ Follow Up
Prospects, Clients and Team

Name	Method of Follow Up/Notes
1. _____	_____
2. _____	_____
3. _____	_____
4. _____	_____
5. _____	_____

☐ Instagram
☐ Facebook

☐ Birthday Acknowledgement
☐ Recorded Training Audio/Video

Win(s) For The Day:

_____

_____

_____

You are radiant.

What You Track Grows ...
So Lets Start Tracking

Date: _____

60 Minutes of Daily Focus

20 Minutes ~ Mindset
Gratitude: Today I'm **Grateful** For..

_____

_____

_____

_____

_____

☐ Gratitude - 1 Minute   ☐ Movement - 5 Minutes
☐ Meditation - 2 Minutes   ☐ Read - 10 Minutes
☐ Affirmations - 2 Minutes

Today's 3 Non Negotiables:

_____

_____

_____

To Do:

1. _____ ☐   4. _____ ☐

2. _____ ☐   5. _____ ☐

3. _____ ☐   6. _____ ☐

Done ☑   Extend ☐/   Delegate ☐○   Remove ☒

20 Minutes ~ Relationship Building
People you introduce your product/service to, new connections and reconnections.

Name	Method of Follow Up/Notes
1. _____	_____
2. _____	_____
3. _____	_____
4. _____	_____
5. _____	_____

20 Minutes ~ Follow Up
Prospects, Clients and Team

Name	Method of Follow Up/Notes
1. _____	_____
2. _____	_____
3. _____	_____
4. _____	_____
5. _____	_____

☐ Instagram   ☐ Birthday Acknowledgement
☐ Facebook   ☐ Recorded Training Audio/Video

Win(s) For The Day:

_____

_____

_____

You are braver than you think.

What You Track Grows ...
So Lets Start Tracking

Date: _____

60 Minutes of Daily Focus

20 Minutes ~ Mindset
Gratitude: Today I'm **Grateful** For..

_____

_____

_____

_____

_____

☐ Gratitude - 1 Minute   ☐ Movement - 5 Minutes

☐ Meditation - 2 Minutes   ☐ Read - 10 Minutes

☐ Affirmations - 2 Minutes

Today's 3 Non Negotiables:

_____

_____

_____

To Do:

1. _____ ☐   4. _____ ☐

2. _____ ☐   5. _____ ☐

3. _____ ☐   6. _____ ☐

| Done ☑ | Extend ☑ | Delegate ◉ | Remove ☒ |

20 Minutes ~ Relationship Building
People you introduce your product/service to, new connections and reconnections.

Name	Method of Follow Up/Notes
1. _____	_____
2. _____	_____
3. _____	_____
4. _____	_____
5. _____	_____

20 Minutes ~ Follow Up
Prospects, Clients and Team

Name	Method of Follow Up/Notes
1. _____	_____
2. _____	_____
3. _____	_____
4. _____	_____
5. _____	_____

☐ Instagram
☐ Facebook

☐ Birthday Acknowledgement
☐ Recorded Training Audio/Video

Win(s) For The Day:

_____

_____

_____

You are such a blessing.

What You Track Grows ...
So Lets Start Tracking

Date: _____

60 Minutes of Daily Focus

20 Minutes ~ Mindset
Gratitude: Today I'm **Grateful** For..

_____

_____

_____

_____

_____

☐ Gratitude - 1 Minute   ☐ Movement - 5 Minutes

☐ Meditation - 2 Minutes   ☐ Read - 10 Minutes

☐ Affirmations - 2 Minutes

Today's 3 Non Negotiables:

_____

_____

_____

To Do:

1. _____ ☐   4. _____ ☐

2. _____ ☐   5. _____ ☐

3. _____ ☐   6. _____ ☐

| Done ☑ | Extend ⧄ | Delegate ◎ | Remove ☒ |

20 Minutes ~ Relationship Building
People you introduce your product/service to, new connections and reconnections.

Name	Method of Follow Up/Notes
1. _____	_____
2. _____	_____
3. _____	_____
4. _____	_____
5. _____	_____

20 Minutes ~ Follow Up
Prospects, Clients and Team

Name	Method of Follow Up/Notes
1. _____	_____
2. _____	_____
3. _____	_____
4. _____	_____
5. _____	_____

☐ Instagram
☐ Facebook

☐ Birthday Acknowledgement
☐ Recorded Training Audio/Video

Win(s) For The Day:

_____

_____

_____

You are powerful.

What You Track Grows ...
So Lets Start Tracking

Date: _____

60 Minutes of Daily Focus

20 Minutes ~ Mindset
Gratitude: Today I'm **Grateful** For..

_____

_____

_____

_____

_____

- ☐ Gratitude - 1 Minute
- ☐ Meditation - 2 Minutes
- ☐ Affirmations - 2 Minutes

- ☐ Movement - 5 Minutes
- ☐ Read - 10 Minutes

Today's 3 Non Negotiables:

_____

_____

_____

To Do:

1. _____ ☐   4. _____ ☐

2. _____ ☐   5. _____ ☐

3. _____ ☐   6. _____ ☐

| Done ☑ | Extend ☑ | Delegate ⊡ | Remove ☒ |

20 Minutes ~ Relationship Building
People you introduce your product/service to, new connections and reconnections.

Name	Method of Follow Up/Notes
1. _____	_____
2. _____	_____
3. _____	_____
4. _____	_____
5. _____	_____

20 Minutes ~ Follow Up
Prospects, Clients and Team

Name	Method of Follow Up/Notes
1. _____	_____
2. _____	_____
3. _____	_____
4. _____	_____
5. _____	_____

☐ Instagram
☐ Facebook

☐ Birthday Acknowledgement
☐ Recorded Training Audio/Video

Win(s) For The Day:

_____

_____

_____

Your smile is contagious.

What You Track Grows ...
So Lets Start Tracking

Date: _____

60 Minutes of Daily Focus

20 Minutes ~ Mindset
Gratitude: Today I'm **Grateful** For..

_____

_____

_____

_____

_____

☐ Gratitude - 1 Minute   ☐ Movement - 5 Minutes

☐ Meditation - 2 Minutes   ☐ Read - 10 Minutes

☐ Affirmations - 2 Minutes

Today's 3 Non Negotiables:

_____

_____

_____

To Do:

1. _____ ☐   4. _____ ☐

2. _____ ☐   5. _____ ☐

3. _____ ☐   6. _____ ☐

| Done ☑ | Extend ☑ | Delegate ◎ | Remove ☒ |

20 Minutes ~ Relationship Building
People you introduce your product/service to, new connections and reconnections.

	Name	Method of Follow Up/Notes
1.	_____	_____
2.	_____	_____
3.	_____	_____
4.	_____	_____
5.	_____	_____

20 Minutes ~ Follow Up
Prospects, Clients and Team

	Name	Method of Follow Up/Notes
1.	_____	_____
2.	_____	_____
3.	_____	_____
4.	_____	_____
5.	_____	_____

☐ Instagram
☐ Facebook

☐ Birthday Acknowledgement
☐ Recorded Training Audio/Video

Win(s) For The Day:

_____

_____

_____

You make the world a better place.

What You Track Grows ...
So Lets Start Tracking

Date: _____

60 Minutes of Daily Focus

20 Minutes ~ Mindset
Gratitude: Today I'm **Grateful** For..

_____

_____

_____

_____

_____

☐ Gratitude - 1 Minute   ☐ Movement - 5 Minutes

☐ Meditation - 2 Minutes   ☐ Read - 10 Minutes

☐ Affirmations - 2 Minutes

Today's 3 Non Negotiables:

_____

_____

_____

To Do:

1. _____ ☐   4. _____ ☐

2. _____ ☐   5. _____ ☐

3. _____ ☐   6. _____ ☐

Done ☑   **Extend** ☑   **Delegate** ◉   **Remove** ☒

20 Minutes ~ Relationship Building
People you introduce your product/service to, new connections and reconnections.

Name | Method of Follow Up/Notes

1. _____   _____
2. _____   _____
3. _____   _____
4. _____   _____
5. _____   _____

20 Minutes ~ Follow Up
Prospects, Clients and Team

Name | Method of Follow Up/Notes

1. _____   _____
2. _____   _____
3. _____   _____
4. _____   _____
5. _____   _____

☐ Instagram   ☐ Birthday Acknowledgement
☐ Facebook   ☐ Recorded Training Audio/Video

Win(s) For The Day:

_____

_____

_____

You have the best ideas.

What You Track Grows ...
So Lets Start Tracking

Date: _____

60 Minutes of Daily Focus

20 Minutes ~ Mindset
Gratitude: Today I'm **Grateful** For..

_____
_____
_____
_____
_____

☐ Gratitude - 1 Minute   ☐ Movement - 5 Minutes
☐ Meditation - 2 Minutes   ☐ Read - 10 Minutes
☐ Affirmations - 2 Minutes

Today's 3 Non Negotiables:

_____
_____
_____

To Do:

1. _____ ☐   4. _____ ☐
2. _____ ☐   5. _____ ☐
3. _____ ☐   6. _____ ☐

| Done ☑ | Extend ⊘ | Delegate ◉ | Remove ☒ |

20 Minutes ~ Relationship Building
People you introduce your product/service to, new connections and reconnections.

Name	Method of Follow Up/Notes
1. _____	_____
2. _____	_____
3. _____	_____
4. _____	_____
5. _____	_____

20 Minutes ~ Follow Up
Prospects, Clients and Team

Name	Method of Follow Up/Notes
1. _____	_____
2. _____	_____
3. _____	_____
4. _____	_____
5. _____	_____

☐ Instagram
☐ Facebook

☐ Birthday Acknowledgement
☐ Recorded Training Audio/Video

Win(s) For The Day:

_____

_____

_____

You are perfect just the way you are.

What You Track Grows ...

So Lets Start Tracking

Date: _____

60 Minutes of Daily Focus

20 Minutes ~ Mindset
Gratitude: Today I'm **Grateful** For..

_____

_____

_____

_____

_____

☐ Gratitude - 1 Minute   ☐ Movement - 5 Minutes

☐ Meditation - 2 Minutes   ☐ Read - 10 Minutes

☐ Affirmations - 2 Minutes

Today's 3 Non Negotiables:

_____

_____

_____

To Do:

1. _____ ☐   4. _____ ☐

2. _____ ☐   5. _____ ☐

3. _____ ☐   6. _____ ☐

| Done ☑ | Extend ☑ | Delegate ◉ | Remove ☒ |

20 Minutes ~ Relationship Building
People you introduce your product/service to, new connections and reconnections.

Name	Method of Follow Up/Notes
1. _____	_____
2. _____	_____
3. _____	_____
4. _____	_____
5. _____	_____

20 Minutes ~ Follow Up
Prospects, Clients and Team

Name	Method of Follow Up/Notes
1. _____	_____
2. _____	_____
3. _____	_____
4. _____	_____
5. _____	_____

☐ Instagram
☐ Facebook

☐ Birthday Acknowledgement
☐ Recorded Training Audio/Video

Win(s) For The Day:

_____

_____

_____

You are magic.

What You Track Grows ...

So Lets Start Tracking

Date: _____

60 Minutes of Daily Focus

20 Minutes ~ Mindset
Gratitude: Today I'm **Grateful** For..

_____

_____

_____

_____

_____

☐ Gratitude - 1 Minute   ☐ Movement - 5 Minutes

☐ Meditation - 2 Minutes   ☐ Read - 10 Minutes

☐ Affirmations - 2 Minutes

Today's 3 Non Negotiables:

_____

_____

_____

To Do:

1. _____ ☐   4. _____ ☐

2. _____ ☐   5. _____ ☐

3. _____ ☐   6. _____ ☐

| Done ☑ | Extend ☑ | Delegate ◉ | Remove ☒ |

20 Minutes ~ Relationship Building

People you introduce your product/service to, new connections and reconnections.

Name	Method of Follow Up/Notes
1. _____	_____
2. _____	_____
3. _____	_____
4. _____	_____
5. _____	_____

20 Minutes ~ Follow Up

Prospects, Clients and Team

Name	Method of Follow Up/Notes
1. _____	_____
2. _____	_____
3. _____	_____
4. _____	_____
5. _____	_____

☐ Instagram
☐ Facebook

☐ Birthday Acknowledgement
☐ Recorded Training Audio/Video

Win(s) For The Day:

_____

_____

_____

You are inspiring.

What You Track Grows ...
So Lets Start Tracking

Date: _____

60 Minutes of Daily Focus

20 Minutes ~ Mindset
Gratitude: Today I'm **Grateful** For..

_____

_____

_____

_____

- ☐ Gratitude - 1 Minute
- ☐ Meditation - 2 Minutes
- ☐ Affirmations - 2 Minutes

- ☐ Movement - 5 Minutes
- ☐ Read - 10 Minutes

Today's 3 Non Negotiables:

_____

_____

_____

To Do:

1. _____ ☐   4. _____ ☐

2. _____ ☐   5. _____ ☐

3. _____ ☐   6. _____ ☐

| Done ☑ | Extend ☑ | Delegate ⊙ | Remove ☒ |

20 Minutes ~ Relationship Building
People you introduce your product/service to, new connections and reconnections.

Name   Method of Follow Up/Notes

1. _____   _____

2. _____   _____

3. _____   _____

4. _____   _____

5. _____   _____

20 Minutes ~ Follow Up
Prospects, Clients and Team

Name   Method of Follow Up/Notes

1. _____   _____

2. _____   _____

3. _____   _____

4. _____   _____

5. _____   _____

☐ Instagram   ☐ Birthday Acknowledgement
☐ Facebook   ☐ Recorded Training Audio/Video

Win(s) For The Day:

_____

_____

_____

You are so worthy of a beautiful life.

What You Track Grows …
So Lets Start Tracking

Date: _____

60 Minutes of Daily Focus

20 Minutes ~ Mindset
Gratitude: Today I'm **Grateful** For..

_____

_____

_____

_____

_____

☐ Gratitude - 1 Minute   ☐ Movement - 5 Minutes

☐ Meditation - 2 Minutes   ☐ Read - 10 Minutes

☐ Affirmations - 2 Minutes

Today's 3 Non Negotiables:

_____

_____

_____

To Do:

1. _____ ☐   4. _____ ☐

2. _____ ☐   5. _____ ☐

3. _____ ☐   6. _____ ☐

Done ☑   Extend ☑   Delegate ◉   Remove ☒

20 Minutes ~ Relationship Building
People you introduce your product/service to, new connections and reconnections.

Name

Method of Follow Up/Notes

1. _____   _____

2. _____   _____

3. _____   _____

4. _____   _____

5. _____   _____

20 Minutes ~ Follow Up
Prospects, Clients and Team

Name

Method of Follow Up/Notes

1. _____   _____

2. _____   _____

3. _____   _____

4. _____   _____

5. _____   _____

☐ Instagram   ☐ Birthday Acknowledgement
☐ Facebook   ☐ Recorded Training Audio/Video

Win(s) For The Day:

_____

_____

_____

You've totally got this.

What You Track Grows ...
So Lets Start Tracking

Date: _____

60 Minutes of Daily Focus

20 Minutes ~ Mindset
Gratitude: Today I'm **Grateful** For..

_____
_____
_____
_____
_____

- ☐ Gratitude - 1 Minute
- ☐ Meditation - 2 Minutes
- ☐ Affirmations - 2 Minutes

- ☐ Movement - 5 Minutes
- ☐ Read - 10 Minutes

Today's 3 Non Negotiables:

_____
_____
_____

To Do:

1. _____ ☐   4. _____ ☐

2. _____ ☐   5. _____ ☐

3. _____ ☐   6. _____ ☐

| Done ☑ | Extend ☑ | Delegate ◉ | Remove ☒ |

20 Minutes ~ Relationship Building
People you introduce your product/service to, new connections and reconnections.

Name	Method of Follow Up/Notes
1. _____	_____
2. _____	_____
3. _____	_____
4. _____	_____
5. _____	_____

20 Minutes ~ Follow Up
Prospects, Clients and Team

Name	Method of Follow Up/Notes
1. _____	_____
2. _____	_____
3. _____	_____
4. _____	_____
5. _____	_____

☐ Instagram
☐ Facebook

☐ Birthday Acknowledgement
☐ Recorded Training Audio/Video

Win(s) For The Day:

_____

_____

_____

You define kind.

What You Track Grows ...
So Lets Start Tracking

Date: _____

60 Minutes of Daily Focus

20 Minutes ~ Mindset
Gratitude: Today I'm **Grateful** For..

_____

_____

_____

_____

_____

☐ Gratitude - 1 Minute   ☐ Movement - 5 Minutes

☐ Meditation - 2 Minutes   ☐ Read - 10 Minutes

☐ Affirmations - 2 Minutes

Today's 3 Non Negotiables:

_____

_____

_____

To Do:

1. _____ ☐   4. _____ ☐

2. _____ ☐   5. _____ ☐

3. _____ ☐   6. _____ ☐

| Done ☑ | Extend ☑ | Delegate ◎ | Remove ☒ |

20 Minutes ~ Relationship Building
People you introduce your product/service to, new connections and reconnections.

Name	Method of Follow Up/Notes
1. _____	_____
2. _____	_____
3. _____	_____
4. _____	_____
5. _____	_____

20 Minutes ~ Follow Up
Prospects, Clients and Team

Name	Method of Follow Up/Notes
1. _____	_____
2. _____	_____
3. _____	_____
4. _____	_____
5. _____	_____

☐ Instagram
☐ Facebook

☐ Birthday Acknowledgement
☐ Recorded Training Audio/Video

Win(s) For The Day:

_____

_____

_____

You are a rockstar.

What You Track Grows ...
So Lets Start Tracking

Date: _____

60 Minutes of Daily Focus

20 Minutes ~ Mindset
Gratitude: Today I'm **Grateful** For..

_____

_____

_____

_____

☐ Gratitude - 1 Minute   ☐ Movement - 5 Minutes

☐ Meditation - 2 Minutes   ☐ Read - 10 Minutes

☐ Affirmations - 2 Minutes

Today's 3 Non Negotiables:

_____

_____

_____

To Do:

1. _____ ☐   4. _____ ☐

2. _____ ☐   5. _____ ☐

3. _____ ☐   6. _____ ☐

| Done ☑ | Extend ☑ | Delegate ☑ | Remove ☒ |

20 Minutes ~ Relationship Building
People you introduce your product/service to, new connections and reconnections.

Name | Method of Follow Up/Notes

1. _____ _____

2. _____ _____

3. _____ _____

4. _____ _____

5. _____ _____

20 Minutes ~ Follow Up
Prospects, Clients and Team

Name | Method of Follow Up/Notes

1. _____ _____

2. _____ _____

3. _____ _____

4. _____ _____

5. _____ _____

☐ Instagram   ☐ Birthday Acknowledgement
☐ Facebook   ☐ Recorded Training Audio/Video

Win(s) For The Day:

_____

_____

_____

More people should be like you.

What You Track Grows ...
So Lets Start Tracking

Date: _____

60 Minutes of Daily Focus

20 Minutes ~ Mindset
Gratitude: Today I'm **Grateful** For..

_____

_____

_____

_____

_____

☐ Gratitude - 1 Minute   ☐ Movement - 5 Minutes

☐ Meditation - 2 Minutes   ☐ Read - 10 Minutes

☐ Affirmations - 2 Minutes

Today's 3 Non Negotiables:

_____

_____

_____

To Do:

1. _____ ☐   4. _____ ☐

2. _____ ☐   5. _____ ☐

3. _____ ☐   6. _____ ☐

| Done ☑ | Extend ☑ | Delegate ◉ | Remove ☒ |

20 Minutes ~ Relationship Building

People you introduce your product/service to, new connections and reconnections.

Name | Method of Follow Up/Notes

1. _____   _____

2. _____   _____

3. _____   _____

4. _____   _____

5. _____   _____

20 Minutes ~ Follow Up

Prospects, Clients and Team

Name | Method of Follow Up/Notes

1. _____   _____

2. _____   _____

3. _____   _____

4. _____   _____

5. _____   _____

☐ Instagram
☐ Facebook

☐ Birthday Acknowledgement
☐ Recorded Training Audio/Video

Win(s) For The Day:

_____

_____

_____

You're doing a great job.

What You Track Grows ...
So Lets Start Tracking

Date: _____

60 Minutes of Daily Focus

20 Minutes ~ Mindset
Gratitude: Today I'm **Grateful** For..

_____

_____

_____

_____

_____

☐ Gratitude - 1 Minute   ☐ Movement - 5 Minutes
☐ Meditation - 2 Minutes   ☐ Read - 10 Minutes
☐ Affirmations - 2 Minutes

Today's 3 Non Negotiables:

_____

_____

_____

To Do:

1. _____ ☐   4. _____ ☐

2. _____ ☐   5. _____ ☐

3. _____ ☐   6. _____ ☐

| Done ☑ | Extend ☑ | Delegate ◙ | Remove ☒ |

20 Minutes ~ Relationship Building
People you introduce your product/service to, new connections and reconnections.

Name	Method of Follow Up/Notes
1. _____	_____
2. _____	_____
3. _____	_____
4. _____	_____
5. _____	_____

20 Minutes ~ Follow Up
Prospects, Clients and Team

Name	Method of Follow Up/Notes
1. _____	_____
2. _____	_____
3. _____	_____
4. _____	_____
5. _____	_____

☐ Instagram   ☐ Birthday Acknowledgement

☐ Facebook   ☐ Recorded Training Audio/Video

Win(s) For The Day:

_____

_____

_____

You are enough.

What You Track Grows ...

So Lets Start Tracking

Date: _____

60 Minutes of Daily Focus

20 Minutes ~ Mindset
Gratitude: Today I'm **Grateful** For..

_____

_____

_____

_____

_____

- ☐ Gratitude - 1 Minute
- ☐ Meditation - 2 Minutes
- ☐ Affirmations - 2 Minutes

- ☐ Movement - 5 Minutes
- ☐ Read - 10 Minutes

Today's 3 Non Negotiables:

_____

_____

_____

To Do:

1. _____ ☐   4. _____ ☐

2. _____ ☐   5. _____ ☐

3. _____ ☐   6. _____ ☐

| Done ☑ | Extend ☑ | Delegate ◙ | Remove ☒ |

20 Minutes ~ Relationship Building
People you introduce your product/service to, new connections and reconnections.

Name | Method of Follow Up/Notes

1. _____   _____

2. _____   _____

3. _____   _____

4. _____   _____

5. _____   _____

20 Minutes ~ Follow Up
Prospects, Clients and Team

Name | Method of Follow Up/Notes

1. _____   _____

2. _____   _____

3. _____   _____

4. _____   _____

5. _____   _____

☐ Instagram   ☐ Birthday Acknowledgement
☐ Facebook   ☐ Recorded Training Audio/Video

Win(s) For The Day:

_____

_____

_____

You always go above and beyond.

What You Track Grows ...
So Lets Start Tracking

Date: _____

60 Minutes of Daily Focus

20 Minutes ~ Mindset
Gratitude: Today I'm **Grateful** For..

_____ _____

_____ _____

_____ _____

_____ _____

_____ _____

☐ Gratitude - 1 Minute   ☐ Movement - 5 Minutes
☐ Meditation - 2 Minutes   ☐ Read - 10 Minutes
☐ Affirmations - 2 Minutes

Today's 3 Non Negotiables:

_____ _____

_____ _____

_____ _____

To Do:

1. _____ ☐   4. _____ ☐

2. _____ ☐   5. _____ ☐

3. _____ ☐   6. _____ ☐

| Done ☑ | Extend ☑ | Delegate ◎ | Remove ☒ |

20 Minutes ~ Relationship Building

People you introduce your product/service to, new connections and reconnections.

Name	Method of Follow Up/Notes
1. _____	_____
2. _____	_____
3. _____	_____
4. _____	_____
5. _____	_____

20 Minutes ~ Follow Up

Prospects, Clients and Team

Name	Method of Follow Up/Notes
1. _____	_____
2. _____	_____
3. _____	_____
4. _____	_____
5. _____	_____

☐ Instagram ☐ Birthday Acknowledgement

☐ Facebook ☐ Recorded Training Audio/Video

Win(s) For The Day:

_____

_____

_____

You are capable of amazing things.

What You Track Grows ...
So Lets Start Tracking

Date: _____

60 Minutes of Daily Focus

20 Minutes ~ Mindset
Gratitude: Today I'm **Grateful** For..

_____

_____

_____

_____

_____

- ☐ Gratitude - 1 Minute
- ☐ Meditation - 2 Minutes
- ☐ Affirmations - 2 Minutes

- ☐ Movement - 5 Minutes
- ☐ Read - 10 Minutes

Today's 3 Non Negotiables:

_____

_____

_____

To Do:

1. _____ ☐
2. _____ ☐
3. _____ ☐

4. _____ ☐
5. _____ ☐
6. _____ ☐

| Done ☑ | Extend ☑ | Delegate ◙ | Remove ☒ |

20 Minutes ~ Relationship Building
People you introduce your product/service to, new connections and reconnections.

Name   Method of Follow Up/Notes

1. _____   _____

2. _____   _____

3. _____   _____

4. _____   _____

5. _____   _____

20 Minutes ~ Follow Up
Prospects, Clients and Team

Name   Method of Follow Up/Notes

1. _____   _____

2. _____   _____

3. _____   _____

4. _____   _____

5. _____   _____

☐ Instagram   ☐ Birthday Acknowledgement
☐ Facebook   ☐ Recorded Training Audio/Video

Win(s) For The Day:

_____

_____

_____

You are capable of amazing things.

What You Track Grows ...
So Lets Start Tracking

Date: _____

60 Minutes of Daily Focus

20 Minutes ~ Mindset
Gratitude: Today I'm **Grateful** For..

_____

_____

_____

_____

☐ Gratitude - 1 Minute   ☐ Movement - 5 Minutes

☐ Meditation - 2 Minutes   ☐ Read - 10 Minutes

☐ Affirmations - 2 Minutes

Today's 3 Non Negotiables:

_____

_____

_____

To Do:

1. _____ ☐   4. _____ ☐

2. _____ ☐   5. _____ ☐

3. _____ ☐   6. _____ ☐

| Done ☑ | Extend ☑ | Delegate ◉ | Remove ☒ |

20 Minutes ~ Relationship Building

People you introduce your product/service to, new connections and reconnections.

Name	Method of Follow Up/Notes
1. _____	_____
2. _____	_____
3. _____	_____
4. _____	_____
5. _____	_____

20 Minutes ~ Follow Up

Prospects, Clients and Team

Name	Method of Follow Up/Notes
1. _____	_____
2. _____	_____
3. _____	_____
4. _____	_____
5. _____	_____

☐ Instagram
☐ Facebook

☐ Birthday Acknowledgement
☐ Recorded Training Audio/Video

Win(s) For The Day:

_____

_____

_____

You are so loved.

What You Track Grows ...
So Lets Start Tracking

Date: _____

60 Minutes of Daily Focus

20 Minutes ~ Mindset
Gratitude: Today I'm **Grateful** For..

_____

_____

_____

_____

_____

☐ Gratitude - 1 Minute   ☐ Movement - 5 Minutes

☐ Meditation - 2 Minutes   ☐ Read - 10 Minutes

☐ Affirmations - 2 Minutes

Today's 3 Non Negotiables:

_____

_____

_____

To Do:

1. _____ ☐   4. _____ ☐

2. _____ ☐   5. _____ ☐

3. _____ ☐   6. _____ ☐

| Done ☑ | Extend ⧄ | Delegate ◉ | Remove ☒ |

20 Minutes ~ Relationship Building
People you introduce your product/service to, new connections and reconnections.

Name	Method of Follow Up/Notes
1. _____	_____
2. _____	_____
3. _____	_____
4. _____	_____
5. _____	_____

20 Minutes ~ Follow Up
Prospects, Clients and Team

Name	Method of Follow Up/Notes
1. _____	_____
2. _____	_____
3. _____	_____
4. _____	_____
5. _____	_____

☐ Instagram
☐ Facebook

☐ Birthday Acknowledgement
☐ Recorded Training Audio/Video

Win(s) For The Day:

_____

_____

_____

Be kind to yourself.

What You Track Grows ...
So Lets Start Tracking

Date: _____

60 Minutes of Daily Focus

20 Minutes ~ Mindset
Gratitude: Today I'm **Grateful** For..

_____

_____

_____

_____

_____

☐ Gratitude - 1 Minute   ☐ Movement - 5 Minutes

☐ Meditation - 2 Minutes   ☐ Read - 10 Minutes

☐ Affirmations - 2 Minutes

Today's 3 Non Negotiables:

_____

_____

_____

To Do:

1. _____ ☐   4. _____ ☐

2. _____ ☐   5. _____ ☐

3. _____ ☐   6. _____ ☐

Done ☑   Extend ☑   Delegate ◎   Remove ☒

20 Minutes ~ Relationship Building
People you introduce your product/service to, new connections and reconnections.

Name	Method of Follow Up/Notes
1. _____	_____
2. _____	_____
3. _____	_____
4. _____	_____
5. _____	_____

20 Minutes ~ Follow Up
Prospects, Clients and Team

Name	Method of Follow Up/Notes
1. _____	_____
2. _____	_____
3. _____	_____
4. _____	_____
5. _____	_____

☐ Instagram
☐ Facebook

☐ Birthday Acknowledgement
☐ Recorded Training Audio/Video

Win(s) For The Day:

_____

_____

_____

Never forget how beautiful you are.

What You Track Grows ...
So Lets Start Tracking

Date: _____

60 Minutes of Daily Focus

20 Minutes ~ Mindset
Gratitude: Today I'm **Grateful** For..

_____

_____

_____

_____

_____

- ☐ Gratitude - 1 Minute
- ☐ Meditation - 2 Minutes
- ☐ Affirmations - 2 Minutes

- ☐ Movement - 5 Minutes
- ☐ Read - 10 Minutes

Today's 3 Non Negotiables:

_____

_____

_____

To Do:

1. _____ ☐   4. _____ ☐

2. _____ ☐   5. _____ ☐

3. _____ ☐   6. _____ ☐

| Done ☑ | Extend ☑ | Delegate ◙ | Remove ☒ |

20 Minutes ~ Relationship Building
People you introduce your product/service to, new connections and reconnections.

Name	Method of Follow Up/Notes
1. _____	_____
2. _____	_____
3. _____	_____
4. _____	_____
5. _____	_____

20 Minutes ~ Follow Up
Prospects, Clients and Team

Name	Method of Follow Up/Notes
1. _____	_____
2. _____	_____
3. _____	_____
4. _____	_____
5. _____	_____

☐ Instagram
☐ Facebook

☐ Birthday Acknowledgement
☐ Recorded Training Audio/Video

Win(s) For The Day:

_____

_____

_____

You look especially lovely today.

What You Track Grows ...
So Lets Start Tracking

Date: _____

60 Minutes of Daily Focus

20 Minutes ~ Mindset
Gratitude: Today I'm **Grateful** For..

_____ _____

_____ _____

_____ _____

_____ _____

_____ _____

☐ Gratitude - 1 Minute   ☐ Movement - 5 Minutes
☐ Meditation - 2 Minutes   ☐ Read - 10 Minutes
☐ Affirmations - 2 Minutes

Today's 3 Non Negotiables:

_____ _____

_____ _____

_____ _____

To Do:

1. _____ ☐   4. _____ ☐

2. _____ ☐   5. _____ ☐

3. _____ ☐   6. _____ ☐

| Done ☑ | Extend ☑ | Delegate ⓞ | Remove ☒ |

20 Minutes ~ Relationship Building
People you introduce your product/service to, new connections and reconnections.

Name

1. _____
2. _____
3. _____
4. _____
5. _____

Method of Follow Up/Notes

_____

_____

_____

_____

_____

20 Minutes ~ Follow Up
Prospects, Clients and Team

Name

1. _____
2. _____
3. _____
4. _____
5. _____

Method of Follow Up/Notes

_____

_____

_____

_____

_____

☐ Instagram
☐ Facebook

☐ Birthday Acknowledgement
☐ Recorded Training Audio/Video

Win(s) For The Day:

_____

_____

_____

Thanks for being you

What You Track Grows ...
So Lets Start Tracking

Date: _____

60 Minutes of Daily Focus

20 Minutes ~ Mindset
Gratitude: Today I'm **Grateful** For..

_____

_____

_____

_____

_____

☐ Gratitude - 1 Minute   ☐ Movement - 5 Minutes

☐ Meditation - 2 Minutes   ☐ Read - 10 Minutes

☐ Affirmations - 2 Minutes

Today's 3 Non Negotiables:

_____

_____

_____

To Do:

1. _____ ☐   4. _____ ☐

2. _____ ☐   5. _____ ☐

3. _____ ☐   6. _____ ☐

| Done ☑ | Extend ☑ | Delegate ◎ | Remove ☒ |

20 Minutes ~ Relationship Building
People you introduce your product/service to, new connections and reconnections.

Name | Method of Follow Up/Notes

1. _____   _____

2. _____   _____

3. _____   _____

4. _____   _____

5. _____   _____

20 Minutes ~ Follow Up
Prospects, Clients and Team

Name | Method of Follow Up/Notes

1. _____   _____

2. _____   _____

3. _____   _____

4. _____   _____

5. _____   _____

☐ Instagram   ☐ Birthday Acknowledgement
☐ Facebook   ☐ Recorded Training Audio/Video

Win(s) For The Day:

_____

_____

_____

Your possibilities are endless.

What You Track Grows ...
So Lets Start Tracking

Date: _____

60 Minutes of Daily Focus

20 Minutes ~ Mindset
Gratitude: Today I'm **Grateful** For..

_____

_____

_____

_____

_____

☐ Gratitude - 1 Minute   ☐ Movement - 5 Minutes

☐ Meditation - 2 Minutes   ☐ Read - 10 Minutes

☐ Affirmations - 2 Minutes

Today's 3 Non Negotiables:

_____

_____

_____

To Do:

1. _____ ☐   4. _____ ☐

2. _____ ☐   5. _____ ☐

3. _____ ☐   6. _____ ☐

| Done ☑ | Extend ☑ | Delegate ☑ | Remove ☒ |

20 Minutes ~ Relationship Building
People you introduce your product/service to, new connections and reconnections.

Name   Method of Follow Up/Notes

1. _____   _____

2. _____   _____

3. _____   _____

4. _____   _____

5. _____   _____

20 Minutes ~ Follow Up
Prospects, Clients and Team

Name   Method of Follow Up/Notes

1. _____   _____

2. _____   _____

3. _____   _____

4. _____   _____

5. _____   _____

☐ Instagram   ☐ Birthday Acknowledgement
☐ Facebook   ☐ Recorded Training Audio/Video

Win(s) For The Day:

_____

_____

_____

You are fabulous.

What You Track Grows ...
So Lets Start Tracking

Date: _____

60 Minutes of Daily Focus

20 Minutes ~ Mindset
Gratitude: Today I'm **Grateful** For..

_____

_____

_____

_____

_____

☐ Gratitude - 1 Minute   ☐ Movement - 5 Minutes

☐ Meditation - 2 Minutes   ☐ Read - 10 Minutes

☐ Affirmations - 2 Minutes

Today's 3 Non Negotiables:

_____

_____

_____

To Do:

1. _____ ☐   4. _____ ☐

2. _____ ☐   5. _____ ☐

3. _____ ☐   6. _____ ☐

| Done ☑ | Extend ☑ | Delegate ⓞ | Remove ☒ |

20 Minutes ~ Relationship Building

People you introduce your product/service to, new connections and reconnections.

Name   Method of Follow Up/Notes

1. _____   _____

2. _____   _____

3. _____   _____

4. _____   _____

5. _____   _____

20 Minutes ~ Follow Up

Prospects, Clients and Team

Name   Method of Follow Up/Notes

1. _____   _____

2. _____   _____

3. _____   _____

4. _____   _____

5. _____   _____

☐ Instagram   ☐ Birthday Acknowledgement
☐ Facebook   ☐ Recorded Training Audio/Video

Win(s) For The Day:

_____

_____

_____

You are so smart.

What You Track Grows ...
So Lets Start Tracking

Date: _____

60 Minutes of Daily Focus

20 Minutes ~ Mindset
Gratitude: Today I'm **Grateful** For..

_____

_____

_____

_____

_____

☐ Gratitude - 1 Minute   ☐ Movement - 5 Minutes

☐ Meditation - 2 Minutes   ☐ Read - 10 Minutes

☐ Affirmations - 2 Minutes

Today's 3 Non Negotiables:

_____

_____

_____

To Do:

1. _____ ☐   4. _____ ☐

2. _____ ☐   5. _____ ☐

3. _____ ☐   6. _____ ☐

Done ☑   Extend ☑   Delegate ◎   Remove ☒

20 Minutes ~ Relationship Building
People you introduce your product/service to, new connections and reconnections.

	Name	Method of Follow Up/Notes
1.	_____	_____
2.	_____	_____
3.	_____	_____
4.	_____	_____
5.	_____	_____

20 Minutes ~ Follow Up
Prospects, Clients and Team

	Name	Method of Follow Up/Notes
1.	_____	_____
2.	_____	_____
3.	_____	_____
4.	_____	_____
5.	_____	_____

☐ Instagram
☐ Facebook

☐ Birthday Acknowledgement
☐ Recorded Training Audio/Video

Win(s) For The Day:

_____

_____

_____

You make the world a better place.

Notes

Notes

Monthly Overview

MONTH

This Month's Goals :

Non-Negotiables :

Stretch Goals :

Important Action Steps/ Events

- ○ ....
- ○ ....
- ○ ....
- ○ ....
- ○ ....
- ○ ....
- ○ ....
- ○ ....
- ○ ....
- ○ ....

SU	M	TU	W	TH	F	SA

Notes

"The reason most people never reach their goals is that they don't define them, or ever seriously consider them as believable or achievable. Winners can tell where they are going, what they plan to do along the way, and whp will be sharing the adventure with them."
- Denis Waitley

30 Conversations
in 30 Days

Write down the names of each NEW person you present your product/service to.
This can be in person, a 1-on-1 meeting, at an event or online (including recorded presentations).
Your goal is at least 30 conversations per month. How close are you?

_____   _____

_____   _____

_____   _____

_____   _____

_____   _____

_____   _____

_____   _____

_____   _____

_____   _____

_____   _____

_____   _____

_____   _____

_____   _____

_____   _____

_____   _____

What You Track Grows ...
So Lets Start Tracking

Date: _____

60 Minutes of Daily Focus

20 Minutes ~ Mindset
Gratitude: Today I'm **Grateful** For..

_____

_____

_____

_____

_____

☐ Gratitude - 1 Minute   ☐ Movement - 5 Minutes

☐ Meditation - 2 Minutes   ☐ Read - 10 Minutes

☐ Affirmations - 2 Minutes

Today's 3 Non Negotiables:

_____

_____

_____

To Do:

1. _____ ☐   4. _____ ☐

2. _____ ☐   5. _____ ☐

3. _____ ☐   6. _____ ☐

| Done ☑ | Extend ☑ | Delegate ◎ | Remove ☒ |

20 Minutes ~ Relationship Building
People you introduce your product/service to, new connections and reconnections.

Name	Method of Follow Up/Notes
1. _____	_____
2. _____	_____
3. _____	_____
4. _____	_____
5. _____	_____

20 Minutes ~ Follow Up
Prospects, Clients and Team

Name	Method of Follow Up/Notes
1. _____	_____
2. _____	_____
3. _____	_____
4. _____	_____
5. _____	_____

☐ Instagram
☐ Facebook

☐ Birthday Acknowledgement
☐ Recorded Training Audio/Video

Win(s) For The Day:

_____

_____

_____

You are one of a kind.

What You Track Grows ...

So Lets Start Tracking

Date: _____

60 Minutes of Daily Focus

20 Minutes ~ Mindset
Gratitude: Today I'm **Grateful** For..

_____

_____

_____

_____

_____

☐ Gratitude - 1 Minute   ☐ Movement - 5 Minutes

☐ Meditation - 2 Minutes   ☐ Read - 10 Minutes

☐ Affirmations - 2 Minutes

Today's 3 Non Negotiables:

_____

_____

_____

To Do:

1. _____ ☐   4. _____ ☐

2. _____ ☐   5. _____ ☐

3. _____ ☐   6. _____ ☐

| Done ☑ | Extend ☑ | Delegate ◙ | Remove ☒ |

20 Minutes ~ Relationship Building
People you introduce your product/service to, new connections and reconnections.

Name	Method of Follow Up/Notes
1. _____	_____
2. _____	_____
3. _____	_____
4. _____	_____
5. _____	_____

20 Minutes ~ Follow Up
Prospects, Clients and Team

Name	Method of Follow Up/Notes
1. _____	_____
2. _____	_____
3. _____	_____
4. _____	_____
5. _____	_____

☐ Instagram
☐ Facebook

☐ Birthday Acknowledgement
☐ Recorded Training Audio/Video

Win(s) For The Day:

_____

_____

_____

You are radiant.

What You Track Grows ...
So Lets Start Tracking

Date: _____

60 Minutes of Daily Focus

20 Minutes ~ Mindset
Gratitude: Today I'm **Grateful** For..

_____

_____

_____

_____

_____

☐ Gratitude - 1 Minute   ☐ Movement - 5 Minutes
☐ Meditation - 2 Minutes   ☐ Read - 10 Minutes
☐ Affirmations - 2 Minutes

Today's 3 Non Negotiables:

_____

_____

_____

To Do:

1. _____ ☐   4. _____ ☐

2. _____ ☐   5. _____ ☐

3. _____ ☐   6. _____ ☐

| Done ☑ | Extend ◫ | Delegate ⊙ | Remove ☒ |

20 Minutes ~ Relationship Building
People you introduce your product/service to, new connections and reconnections.

	Name	Method of Follow Up/Notes
1.	_____	_____
2.	_____	_____
3.	_____	_____
4.	_____	_____
5.	_____	_____

20 Minutes ~ Follow Up
Prospects, Clients and Team

	Name	Method of Follow Up/Notes
1.	_____	_____
2.	_____	_____
3.	_____	_____
4.	_____	_____
5.	_____	_____

☐ Instagram
☐ Facebook

☐ Birthday Acknowledgement
☐ Recorded Training Audio/Video

Win(s) For The Day:

_____

_____

_____

You are braver than you think.

What You Track Grows ...
So Lets Start Tracking

Date: _____

60 Minutes of Daily Focus

20 Minutes ~ Mindset
Gratitude: Today I'm **Grateful** For..

_____

_____

_____

_____

☐ Gratitude - 1 Minute   ☐ Movement - 5 Minutes
☐ Meditation - 2 Minutes   ☐ Read - 10 Minutes
☐ Affirmations - 2 Minutes

Today's 3 Non Negotiables:

_____

_____

_____

To Do:

1. _____ ☐   4. _____ ☐

2. _____ ☐   5. _____ ☐

3. _____ ☐   6. _____ ☐

| Done ☑ | Extend ☑ | Delegate ◉ | Remove ☒ |

20 Minutes ~ Relationship Building
People you introduce your product/service to, new connections and reconnections.

Name   Method of Follow Up/Notes

1. _____   _____

2. _____   _____

3. _____   _____

4. _____   _____

5. _____   _____

20 Minutes ~ Follow Up
Prospects, Clients and Team

Name   Method of Follow Up/Notes

1. _____   _____

2. _____   _____

3. _____   _____

4. _____   _____

5. _____   _____

☐ Instagram   ☐ Birthday Acknowledgement
☐ Facebook   ☐ Recorded Training Audio/Video

Win(s) For The Day:

_____

_____

_____

You are such a blessing.

What You Track Grows ...
So Lets Start Tracking

Date: _____

60 Minutes of Daily Focus

20 Minutes ~ Mindset
Gratitude: Today I'm **Grateful** For..

_____

_____

_____

_____

_____

☐ Gratitude - 1 Minute   ☐ Movement - 5 Minutes

☐ Meditation - 2 Minutes   ☐ Read - 10 Minutes

☐ Affirmations - 2 Minutes

Today's 3 Non Negotiables:

_____

_____

_____

To Do:

1. _____ ☐   4. _____ ☐

2. _____ ☐   5. _____ ☐

3. _____ ☐   6. _____ ☐

Done ☑   Extend ☑   Delegate ◉   Remove ☒

20 Minutes ~ Relationship Building
People you introduce your product/service to, new connections and reconnections.

Name

Method of Follow Up/Notes

1. _____   _____

2. _____   _____

3. _____   _____

4. _____   _____

5. _____   _____

20 Minutes ~ Follow Up
Prospects, Clients and Team

Name

Method of Follow Up/Notes

1. _____   _____

2. _____   _____

3. _____   _____

4. _____   _____

5. _____   _____

☐ Instagram   ☐ Birthday Acknowledgement
☐ Facebook   ☐ Recorded Training Audio/Video

Win(s) For The Day:

_____

_____

_____

You are powerful.

What You Track Grows ...
So Lets Start Tracking

Date: _____

60 Minutes of Daily Focus

20 Minutes ~ Mindset
Gratitude: Today I'm **Grateful** For..

_____   _____

_____   _____

_____   _____

_____   _____

_____   _____

☐ Gratitude - 1 Minute   ☐ Movement - 5 Minutes
☐ Meditation - 2 Minutes   ☐ Read - 10 Minutes
☐ Affirmations - 2 Minutes

Today's 3 Non Negotiables:

_____   _____

_____   _____

_____   _____

To Do:

1. _____ ☐   4. _____ ☐

2. _____ ☐   5. _____ ☐

3. _____ ☐   6. _____ ☐

| Done ☑ | Extend ☑ | Delegate ◙ | Remove ☒ |

20 Minutes ~ Relationship Building
People you introduce your product/service to, new connections and reconnections.

Name	Method of Follow Up/Notes
1. _____	_____
2. _____	_____
3. _____	_____
4. _____	_____
5. _____	_____

20 Minutes ~ Follow Up
Prospects, Clients and Team

Name	Method of Follow Up/Notes
1. _____	_____
2. _____	_____
3. _____	_____
4. _____	_____
5. _____	_____

☐ Instagram
☐ Facebook

☐ Birthday Acknowledgement
☐ Recorded Training Audio/Video

Win(s) For The Day:

_____

_____

_____

Your smile is contagious.

What You Track Grows ...
So Lets Start Tracking

Date: _____

60 Minutes of Daily Focus

20 Minutes ~ Mindset
Gratitude: Today I'm **Grateful** For..

_____

_____

_____

_____

_____

☐ Gratitude - 1 Minute   ☐ Movement - 5 Minutes

☐ Meditation - 2 Minutes   ☐ Read - 10 Minutes

☐ Affirmations - 2 Minutes

Today's 3 Non Negotiables:

_____

_____

_____

To Do:

1. _____ ☐   4. _____ ☐

2. _____ ☐   5. _____ ☐

3. _____ ☐   6. _____ ☐

| Done ☑ | Extend ☑ | Delegate ⊙ | Remove ☒ |

20 Minutes ~ Relationship Building
People you introduce your product/service to, new connections and reconnections.

Name | Method of Follow Up/Notes

1. _____   _____

2. _____   _____

3. _____   _____

4. _____   _____

5. _____   _____

20 Minutes ~ Follow Up
Prospects, Clients and Team

Name | Method of Follow Up/Notes

1. _____   _____

2. _____   _____

3. _____   _____

4. _____   _____

5. _____   _____

☐ Instagram   ☐ Birthday Acknowledgement
☐ Facebook   ☐ Recorded Training Audio/Video

Win(s) For The Day:

_____

_____

_____

You make the world a better place.

What You Track Grows ...

So Lets Start Tracking

Date: _____

60 Minutes of Daily Focus

20 Minutes ~ Mindset
Gratitude: Today I'm **Grateful** For..

_____

_____

_____

_____

_____

☐ Gratitude - 1 Minute   ☐ Movement - 5 Minutes

☐ Meditation - 2 Minutes   ☐ Read - 10 Minutes

☐ Affirmations - 2 Minutes

Today's 3 Non Negotiables:

_____

_____

_____

To Do:

1. _____ ☐   4. _____ ☐

2. _____ ☐   5. _____ ☐

3. _____ ☐   6. _____ ☐

| Done ☑ | Extend ⊘ | Delegate ⊙ | Remove ⊠ |

20 Minutes ~ Relationship Building
People you introduce your product/service to, new connections and reconnections.

Name | Method of Follow Up/Notes

1. _____   _____

2. _____   _____

3. _____   _____

4. _____   _____

5. _____   _____

20 Minutes ~ Follow Up
Prospects, Clients and Team

Name | Method of Follow Up/Notes

1. _____   _____

2. _____   _____

3. _____   _____

4. _____   _____

5. _____   _____

☐ Instagram   ☐ Birthday Acknowledgement
☐ Facebook   ☐ Recorded Training Audio/Video

Win(s) For The Day:

_____

_____

_____

You have the best ideas.

What You Track Grows ...
So Lets Start Tracking

Date: _____

60 Minutes of Daily Focus

20 Minutes ~ Mindset
Gratitude: Today I'm **Grateful** For..

_____

_____

_____

_____

_____

☐ Gratitude - 1 Minute   ☐ Movement - 5 Minutes

☐ Meditation - 2 Minutes   ☐ Read - 10 Minutes

☐ Affirmations - 2 Minutes

Today's 3 Non Negotiables:

_____

_____

_____

To Do:

1. _____ ☐   4. _____ ☐

2. _____ ☐   5. _____ ☐

3. _____ ☐   6. _____ ☐

Done ☑   **Extend** ☑   **Delegate** ◉   **Remove** ☒

20 Minutes ~ Relationship Building

People you introduce your product/service to, new connections and reconnections.

Name	Method of Follow Up/Notes
1. _____	_____
2. _____	_____
3. _____	_____
4. _____	_____
5. _____	_____

20 Minutes ~ Follow Up

Prospects, Clients and Team

Name	Method of Follow Up/Notes
1. _____	_____
2. _____	_____
3. _____	_____
4. _____	_____
5. _____	_____

☐ Instagram
☐ Facebook

☐ Birthday Acknowledgement
☐ Recorded Training Audio/Video

Win(s) For The Day:

_____

_____

_____

You are perfect just the way you are.

What You Track Grows ...
So Lets Start Tracking

Date: _____

60 Minutes of Daily Focus

20 Minutes ~ Mindset
Gratitude: Today I'm **Grateful** For..

_____

_____

_____

_____

_____

☐ Gratitude - 1 Minute   ☐ Movement - 5 Minutes

☐ Meditation - 2 Minutes   ☐ Read - 10 Minutes

☐ Affirmations - 2 Minutes

Today's 3 Non Negotiables:

_____

_____

_____

To Do:

1. _____ ☐   4. _____ ☐

2. _____ ☐   5. _____ ☐

3. _____ ☐   6. _____ ☐

| Done ☑ | Extend ☐ | Delegate ⊡ | Remove ☒ |

20 Minutes ~ Relationship Building
People you introduce your product/service to, new connections and reconnections.

Name	Method of Follow Up/Notes
1. _____	_____
2. _____	_____
3. _____	_____
4. _____	_____
5. _____	_____

20 Minutes ~ Follow Up
Prospects, Clients and Team

Name	Method of Follow Up/Notes
1. _____	_____
2. _____	_____
3. _____	_____
4. _____	_____
5. _____	_____

☐ Instagram
☐ Facebook

☐ Birthday Acknowledgement
☐ Recorded Training Audio/Video

Win(s) For The Day:

_____

_____

_____

You are magic.

What You Track Grows ...
So Lets Start Tracking

Date: _____

60 Minutes of Daily Focus

20 Minutes ~ Mindset
Gratitude: Today I'm *Grateful* For..

_____

_____

_____

_____

_____

☐ Gratitude - 1 Minute   ☐ Movement - 5 Minutes

☐ Meditation - 2 Minutes   ☐ Read - 10 Minutes

☐ Affirmations - 2 Minutes

Today's 3 Non Negotiables:

_____

_____

_____

To Do:

1. _____ ☐   4. _____ ☐

2. _____ ☐   5. _____ ☐

3. _____ ☐   6. _____ ☐

| Done ☑ | Extend ⊘ | Delegate ⊙ | Remove ⊠ |

20 Minutes ~ Relationship Building

People you introduce your product/service to, new connections and reconnections.

Name   Method of Follow Up/Notes

1. _____   _____

2. _____   _____

3. _____   _____

4. _____   _____

5. _____   _____

20 Minutes ~ Follow Up

Prospects, Clients and Team

Name   Method of Follow Up/Notes

1. _____   _____

2. _____   _____

3. _____   _____

4. _____   _____

5. _____   _____

☐ Instagram   ☐ Birthday Acknowledgement
☐ Facebook   ☐ Recorded Training Audio/Video

Win(s) For The Day:

_____

_____

_____

You are inspiring.

What You Track Grows ...

So Lets Start Tracking

Date: _____

60 Minutes of Daily Focus

20 Minutes ~ Mindset
Gratitude: Today I'm **Grateful** For..

_____ _____

_____ _____

_____ _____

_____ _____

_____

☐ Gratitude - 1 Minute   ☐ Movement - 5 Minutes

☐ Meditation - 2 Minutes   ☐ Read - 10 Minutes

☐ Affirmations - 2 Minutes

Today's 3 Non Negotiables:

_____ _____

_____ _____

_____ _____

To Do:

1. _____ ☐   4. _____ ☐

2. _____ ☐   5. _____ ☐

3. _____ ☐   6. _____ ☐

| Done ☑ | Extend ☑ | Delegate ☑ | Remove ☒ |

20 Minutes ~ Relationship Building

People you introduce your product/service to, new connections and reconnections.

Name   Method of Follow Up/Notes

1. _____   _____

2. _____   _____

3. _____   _____

4. _____   _____

5. _____   _____

20 Minutes ~ Follow Up

Prospects, Clients and Team

Name   Method of Follow Up/Notes

1. _____   _____

2. _____   _____

3. _____   _____

4. _____   _____

5. _____   _____

☐ Instagram   ☐ Birthday Acknowledgement
☐ Facebook   ☐ Recorded Training Audio/Video

Win(s) For The Day:

_____

_____

_____

You are so worthy of a beautiful life.

What You Track Grows ...
So Lets Start Tracking

Date: _____

60 Minutes of Daily Focus

20 Minutes ~ Mindset
Gratitude: Today I'm **Grateful** For..

_____

_____

_____

_____

_____

☐ Gratitude - 1 Minute   ☐ Movement - 5 Minutes

☐ Meditation - 2 Minutes   ☐ Read - 10 Minutes

☐ Affirmations - 2 Minutes

Today's 3 Non Negotiables:

_____

_____

_____

To Do:

1. _____ ☐   4. _____ ☐

2. _____ ☐   5. _____ ☐

3. _____ ☐   6. _____ ☐

| Done ☑ | Extend ☑ | Delegate ⊡ | Remove ☒ |

20 Minutes ~ Relationship Building

People you introduce your product/service to, new connections and reconnections.

Name   Method of Follow Up/Notes

1. _____   _____

2. _____   _____

3. _____   _____

4. _____   _____

5. _____   _____

20 Minutes ~ Follow Up

Prospects, Clients and Team

Name   Method of Follow Up/Notes

1. _____   _____

2. _____   _____

3. _____   _____

4. _____   _____

5. _____   _____

☐ Instagram   ☐ Birthday Acknowledgement
☐ Facebook   ☐ Recorded Training Audio/Video

Win(s) For The Day:

_____

_____

_____

You've totally got this.

What You Track Grows ...
So Lets Start Tracking

Date: _____

60 Minutes of Daily Focus

20 Minutes ~ Mindset
Gratitude: Today I'm **Grateful** For..

_____

_____

_____

_____

_____

☐ Gratitude - 1 Minute   ☐ Movement - 5 Minutes

☐ Meditation - 2 Minutes   ☐ Read - 10 Minutes

☐ Affirmations - 2 Minutes

Today's 3 Non Negotiables:

_____

_____

_____

To Do:

1. _____ ☐   4. _____ ☐

2. _____ ☐   5. _____ ☐

3. _____ ☐   6. _____ ☐

| Done ☑ | Extend ☐/ | Delegate ◎ | Remove ☒ |

20 Minutes ~ Relationship Building
People you introduce your product/service to, new connections and reconnections.

	Name	Method of Follow Up/Notes
1.	_____	_____
2.	_____	_____
3.	_____	_____
4.	_____	_____
5.	_____	_____

20 Minutes ~ Follow Up
Prospects, Clients and Team

	Name	Method of Follow Up/Notes
1.	_____	_____
2.	_____	_____
3.	_____	_____
4.	_____	_____
5.	_____	_____

☐ Instagram   ☐ Birthday Acknowledgement
☐ Facebook   ☐ Recorded Training Audio/Video

Win(s) For The Day:

_____
_____
_____

You define kind.

What You Track Grows ...
So Lets Start Tracking

Date: _____

60 Minutes of Daily Focus

20 Minutes ~ Mindset
Gratitude: Today I'm **Grateful** For..

_____

_____

_____

_____

_____

☐ Gratitude - 1 Minute   ☐ Movement - 5 Minutes

☐ Meditation - 2 Minutes   ☐ Read - 10 Minutes

☐ Affirmations - 2 Minutes

Today's 3 Non Negotiables:

_____

_____

_____

To Do:

1. _____ ☐   4. _____ ☐

2. _____ ☐   5. _____ ☐

3. _____ ☐   6. _____ ☐

Done ☑   Extend ☑   Delegate ⧀   Remove ☒

20 Minutes ~ Relationship Building
People you introduce your product/service to, new connections and reconnections.

Name   Method of Follow Up/Notes

1. _____   _____

2. _____   _____

3. _____   _____

4. _____   _____

5. _____   _____

20 Minutes ~ Follow Up
Prospects, Clients and Team

Name   Method of Follow Up/Notes

1. _____   _____

2. _____   _____

3. _____   _____

4. _____   _____

5. _____   _____

☐ Instagram   ☐ Birthday Acknowledgement
☐ Facebook   ☐ Recorded Training Audio/Video

Win(s) For The Day:

_____

_____

_____

You are a rockstar.

What You Track Grows ...
So Lets Start Tracking

Date: _____

60 Minutes of Daily Focus

20 Minutes ~ Mindset
Gratitude: Today I'm **Grateful** For..

_____

_____

_____

_____

_____

☐ Gratitude - 1 Minute   ☐ Movement - 5 Minutes
☐ Meditation - 2 Minutes   ☐ Read - 10 Minutes
☐ Affirmations - 2 Minutes

Today's 3 Non Negotiables:

_____

_____

_____

To Do:

1. _____ ☐   4. _____ ☐

2. _____ ☐   5. _____ ☐

3. _____ ☐   6. _____ ☐

| Done ☑ | Extend ☑ | Delegate ◎ | Remove ☒ |

20 Minutes ~ Relationship Building
People you introduce your product/service to, new connections and reconnections.

Name	Method of Follow Up/Notes
1. _____	_____
2. _____	_____
3. _____	_____
4. _____	_____
5. _____	_____

20 Minutes ~ Follow Up
Prospects, Clients and Team

Name	Method of Follow Up/Notes
1. _____	_____
2. _____	_____
3. _____	_____
4. _____	_____
5. _____	_____

☐ Instagram
☐ Facebook

☐ Birthday Acknowledgement
☐ Recorded Training Audio/Video

Win(s) For The Day:

_____

_____

_____

More people should be like you.

What You Track Grows ...
So Lets Start Tracking

Date: _____

60 Minutes of Daily Focus

20 Minutes ~ Mindset
Gratitude: Today I'm **Grateful** For..

_____

_____

_____

_____

_____

☐ Gratitude - 1 Minute   ☐ Movement - 5 Minutes

☐ Meditation - 2 Minutes   ☐ Read - 10 Minutes

☐ Affirmations - 2 Minutes

Today's 3 Non Negotiables:

_____

_____

_____

To Do:

1. _____ ☐   4. _____ ☐

2. _____ ☐   5. _____ ☐

3. _____ ☐   6. _____ ☐

| Done ☑ | Extend ☑ | Delegate ◉ | Remove ☒ |

20 Minutes ~ Relationship Building
People you introduce your product/service to, new connections and reconnections.

Name

Method of Follow Up/Notes

1. _____   _____

2. _____   _____

3. _____   _____

4. _____   _____

5. _____   _____

20 Minutes ~ Follow Up
Prospects, Clients and Team

Name

Method of Follow Up/Notes

1. _____   _____

2. _____   _____

3. _____   _____

4. _____   _____

5. _____   _____

☐ Instagram   ☐ Birthday Acknowledgement
☐ Facebook   ☐ Recorded Training Audio/Video

Win(s) For The Day:

_____

_____

_____

You're doing a great job.

What You Track Grows ...
So Lets Start Tracking

Date: _____

60 Minutes of Daily Focus

20 Minutes ~ Mindset
Gratitude: Today I'm **Grateful** For..

_____

_____

_____

_____

_____

☐ Gratitude - 1 Minute   ☐ Movement - 5 Minutes

☐ Meditation - 2 Minutes   ☐ Read - 10 Minutes

☐ Affirmations - 2 Minutes

Today's 3 Non Negotiables:

_____

_____

_____

To Do:

1. _____ ☐   4. _____ ☐

2. _____ ☐   5. _____ ☐

3. _____ ☐   6. _____ ☐

| Done ☑ | Extend ⊘ | Delegate ⊙ | Remove ☒ |

20 Minutes ~ Relationship Building
People you introduce your product/service to, new connections and reconnections.

Name   Method of Follow Up/Notes

1. _____   _____

2. _____   _____

3. _____   _____

4. _____   _____

5. _____   _____

20 Minutes ~ Follow Up
Prospects, Clients and Team

Name   Method of Follow Up/Notes

1. _____   _____

2. _____   _____

3. _____   _____

4. _____   _____

5. _____   _____

☐ Instagram   ☐ Birthday Acknowledgement
☐ Facebook   ☐ Recorded Training Audio/Video

Win(s) For The Day:

_____

_____

_____

You are enough.

What You Track Grows ...
So Lets Start Tracking

Date: _____

60 Minutes of Daily Focus

20 Minutes ~ Mindset
Gratitude: Today I'm **Grateful** For..

_____

_____

_____

_____

_____

- ☐ Gratitude - 1 Minute
- ☐ Meditation - 2 Minutes
- ☐ Affirmations - 2 Minutes

- ☐ Movement - 5 Minutes
- ☐ Read - 10 Minutes

Today's 3 Non Negotiables:

_____

_____

_____

To Do:

1. _____ ☐   4. _____ ☐

2. _____ ☐   5. _____ ☐

3. _____ ☐   6. _____ ☐

| Done ☑ | Extend ☑ | Delegate ◙ | Remove ☒ |

20 Minutes ~ Relationship Building
People you introduce your product/service to, new connections and reconnections.

Name   Method of Follow Up/Notes

1. _____   _____

2. _____   _____

3. _____   _____

4. _____   _____

5. _____   _____

20 Minutes ~ Follow Up
Prospects, Clients and Team

Name   Method of Follow Up/Notes

1. _____   _____

2. _____   _____

3. _____   _____

4. _____   _____

5. _____   _____

☐ Instagram   ☐ Birthday Acknowledgement
☐ Facebook   ☐ Recorded Training Audio/Video

Win(s) For The Day:

_____

_____

_____

You always go above and beyond.

What You Track Grows …
So Lets Start Tracking

Date: _____

60 Minutes of Daily Focus

20 Minutes ~ Mindset
Gratitude: Today I'm *Grateful* For..

_____

_____

_____

_____

_____

☐ Gratitude - 1 Minute   ☐ Movement - 5 Minutes
☐ Meditation - 2 Minutes   ☐ Read - 10 Minutes
☐ Affirmations - 2 Minutes

Today's 3 Non Negotiables:

_____

_____

_____

To Do:

1. _____ ☐   4. _____ ☐

2. _____ ☐   5. _____ ☐

3. _____ ☐   6. _____ ☐

| Done ☑ | Extend ☑ | Delegate ◙ | Remove ☒ |

20 Minutes ~ Relationship Building

People you introduce your product/service to, new connections and reconnections.

Name   Method of Follow Up/Notes

1. _____   _____

2. _____   _____

3. _____   _____

4. _____   _____

5. _____   _____

20 Minutes ~ Follow Up

Prospects, Clients and Team

Name   Method of Follow Up/Notes

1. _____   _____

2. _____   _____

3. _____   _____

4. _____   _____

5. _____   _____

☐ Instagram   ☐ Birthday Acknowledgement
☐ Facebook   ☐ Recorded Training Audio/Video

Win(s) For The Day:

_____

_____

You are capable of amazing things.

What You Track Grows ...
So Lets Start Tracking

Date: _____

60 Minutes of Daily Focus

20 Minutes ~ Mindset
Gratitude: Today I'm **Grateful** For..

_____

_____

_____

_____

_____

☐ Gratitude - 1 Minute   ☐ Movement - 5 Minutes

☐ Meditation - 2 Minutes   ☐ Read - 10 Minutes

☐ Affirmations - 2 Minutes

Today's 3 Non Negotiables:

_____

_____

_____

To Do:

1. _____ ☐   4. _____ ☐

2. _____ ☐   5. _____ ☐

3. _____ ☐   6. _____ ☐

Done ☑   Extend ☑   Delegate ◙   Remove ☒

20 Minutes ~ Relationship Building
People you introduce your product/service to, new connections and reconnections.

Name	Method of Follow Up/Notes
1. _____	_____
2. _____	_____
3. _____	_____
4. _____	_____
5. _____	_____

20 Minutes ~ Follow Up
Prospects, Clients and Team

Name	Method of Follow Up/Notes
1. _____	_____
2. _____	_____
3. _____	_____
4. _____	_____
5. _____	_____

☐ Instagram
☐ Facebook

☐ Birthday Acknowledgement
☐ Recorded Training Audio/Video

Win(s) For The Day:

_____

_____

_____

You are capable of amazing things.

What You Track Grows ...

So Lets Start Tracking

Date: _____

60 Minutes of Daily Focus

20 Minutes ~ Mindset
Gratitude: Today I'm **Grateful** For..

_____

_____

_____

_____

_____

☐ Gratitude - 1 Minute   ☐ Movement - 5 Minutes

☐ Meditation - 2 Minutes   ☐ Read - 10 Minutes

☐ Affirmations - 2 Minutes

Today's 3 Non Negotiables:

_____

_____

_____

To Do:

1. _____ ☐   4. _____ ☐

2. _____ ☐   5. _____ ☐

3. _____ ☐   6. _____ ☐

Done ☑   Extend ☑   Delegate ☑   Remove ☒

20 Minutes ~ Relationship Building
People you introduce your product/service to, new connections and reconnections.

Name	Method of Follow Up/Notes
1. _____	_____
2. _____	_____
3. _____	_____
4. _____	_____
5. _____	_____

20 Minutes ~ Follow Up
Prospects, Clients and Team

Name	Method of Follow Up/Notes
1. _____	_____
2. _____	_____
3. _____	_____
4. _____	_____
5. _____	_____

☐ Instagram
☐ Facebook

☐ Birthday Acknowledgement
☐ Recorded Training Audio/Video

Win(s) For The Day:

_____

_____

_____

You are so loved.

What You Track Grows ...
So Lets Start Tracking

Date: _____

60 Minutes of Daily Focus

20 Minutes ~ Mindset
Gratitude: Today I'm *Grateful* For..

_____

_____

_____

_____

_____

- ☐ Gratitude - 1 Minute
- ☐ Meditation - 2 Minutes
- ☐ Affirmations - 2 Minutes

- ☐ Movement - 5 Minutes
- ☐ Read - 10 Minutes

Today's 3 Non Negotiables:

_____

_____

_____

To Do:

1. _____ ☐   4. _____ ☐

2. _____ ☐   5. _____ ☐

3. _____ ☐   6. _____ ☐

| Done ☑ | Extend ⊘ | Delegate ⊚ | Remove ☒ |

20 Minutes ~ Relationship Building
People you introduce your product/service to, new connections and reconnections.

Name | Method of Follow Up/Notes

1. _____   _____

2. _____   _____

3. _____   _____

4. _____   _____

5. _____   _____

20 Minutes ~ Follow Up
Prospects, Clients and Team

Name | Method of Follow Up/Notes

1. _____   _____

2. _____   _____

3. _____   _____

4. _____   _____

5. _____   _____

☐ Instagram
☐ Facebook

☐ Birthday Acknowledgement
☐ Recorded Training Audio/Video

Win(s) For The Day:

_____

_____

_____

Be kind to yourself.

What You Track Grows ...
So Lets Start Tracking

Date: _____

60 Minutes of Daily Focus

20 Minutes ~ Mindset
Gratitude: Today I'm **Grateful** For..

_____

_____

_____

_____

_____

☐ Gratitude - 1 Minute   ☐ Movement - 5 Minutes

☐ Meditation - 2 Minutes   ☐ Read - 10 Minutes

☐ Affirmations - 2 Minutes

Today's 3 Non Negotiables:

_____

_____

_____

To Do:

1. _____ ☐   4. _____ ☐

2. _____ ☐   5. _____ ☐

3. _____ ☐   6. _____ ☐

| Done ☑ | Extend ☑ | Delegate ◙ | Remove ☒ |

20 Minutes ~ Relationship Building
People you introduce your product/service to, new connections and reconnections.

Name   Method of Follow Up/Notes

1. _____   _____

2. _____   _____

3. _____   _____

4. _____   _____

5. _____   _____

20 Minutes ~ Follow Up
Prospects, Clients and Team

Name   Method of Follow Up/Notes

1. _____   _____

2. _____   _____

3. _____   _____

4. _____   _____

5. _____   _____

☐ Instagram   ☐ Birthday Acknowledgement
☐ Facebook   ☐ Recorded Training Audio/Video

Win(s) For The Day:

_____

_____

_____

Never forget how beautiful you are.

What You Track Grows …
So Lets Start Tracking

Date: _____

60 Minutes of Daily Focus

20 Minutes ~ Mindset
Gratitude: Today I'm **Grateful** For..

_____

_____

_____

_____

_____

- ☐ Gratitude - 1 Minute
- ☐ Meditation - 2 Minutes
- ☐ Affirmations - 2 Minutes

- ☐ Movement - 5 Minutes
- ☐ Read - 10 Minutes

Today's 3 Non Negotiables:

_____

_____

_____

To Do:

1. _____ ☐   4. _____ ☐

2. _____ ☐   5. _____ ☐

3. _____ ☐   6. _____ ☐

| Done ☑ | Extend ☑ | Delegate ◎ | Remove ☒ |

20 Minutes ~ Relationship Building

People you introduce your product/service to, new connections and reconnections.

	Name	Method of Follow Up/Notes
1.	_____	_____
2.	_____	_____
3.	_____	_____
4.	_____	_____
5.	_____	_____

20 Minutes ~ Follow Up

Prospects, Clients and Team

	Name	Method of Follow Up/Notes
1.	_____	_____
2.	_____	_____
3.	_____	_____
4.	_____	_____
5.	_____	_____

☐ Instagram   ☐ Birthday Acknowledgement
☐ Facebook   ☐ Recorded Training Audio/Video

Win(s) For The Day:

_____

_____

_____

You look especially lovely today.

What You Track Grows ...
So Lets Start Tracking

Date: _____

60 Minutes of Daily Focus

20 Minutes ~ Mindset
Gratitude: Today I'm **Grateful** For..

_____

_____

_____

_____

_____

☐ Gratitude - 1 Minute   ☐ Movement - 5 Minutes

☐ Meditation - 2 Minutes   ☐ Read - 10 Minutes

☐ Affirmations - 2 Minutes

Today's 3 Non Negotiables:

_____

_____

_____

To Do:

1. _____ ☐   4. _____ ☐

2. _____ ☐   5. _____ ☐

3. _____ ☐   6. _____ ☐

| Done ☑ | Extend ☑ | Delegate ◙ | Remove ☒ |

20 Minutes ~ Relationship Building
People you introduce your product/service to, new connections and reconnections.

Name	Method of Follow Up/Notes
1. _____	_____
2. _____	_____
3. _____	_____
4. _____	_____
5. _____	_____

20 Minutes ~ Follow Up
Prospects, Clients and Team

Name	Method of Follow Up/Notes
1. _____	_____
2. _____	_____
3. _____	_____
4. _____	_____
5. _____	_____

☐ Instagram
☐ Facebook

☐ Birthday Acknowledgement
☐ Recorded Training Audio/Video

Win(s) For The Day:

_____

_____

_____

Thanks for being you   .

What You Track Grows ...
So Lets Start Tracking

Date: _____

60 Minutes of Daily Focus

20 Minutes ~ Mindset
Gratitude: Today I'm **Grateful** For..

_____

_____

_____

_____

_____

☐ Gratitude - 1 Minute   ☐ Movement - 5 Minutes

☐ Meditation - 2 Minutes   ☐ Read - 10 Minutes

☐ Affirmations - 2 Minutes

Today's 3 Non Negotiables:

_____

_____

_____

To Do:

1. _____ ☐   4. _____ ☐

2. _____ ☐   5. _____ ☐

3. _____ ☐   6. _____ ☐

| Done ☑ | Extend ⊘ | Delegate ⊚ | Remove ☒ |

20 Minutes ~ Relationship Building
People you introduce your product/service to, new connections and reconnections.

Name	Method of Follow Up/Notes
1. _____	_____
2. _____	_____
3. _____	_____
4. _____	_____
5. _____	_____

20 Minutes ~ Follow Up
Prospects, Clients and Team

Name	Method of Follow Up/Notes
1. _____	_____
2. _____	_____
3. _____	_____
4. _____	_____
5. _____	_____

☐ Instagram
☐ Facebook

☐ Birthday Acknowledgement
☐ Recorded Training Audio/Video

Win(s) For The Day:

_____

_____

_____

Your possibilities are endless.

What You Track Grows ...
So Lets Start Tracking

Date: _____

60 Minutes of Daily Focus

20 Minutes ~ Mindset
Gratitude: Today I'm **Grateful** For..

_____

_____

_____

_____

_____

☐ Gratitude - 1 Minute   ☐ Movement - 5 Minutes

☐ Meditation - 2 Minutes   ☐ Read - 10 Minutes

☐ Affirmations - 2 Minutes

Today's 3 Non Negotiables:

_____

_____

_____

To Do:

1. _____ ☐   4. _____ ☐

2. _____ ☐   5. _____ ☐

3. _____ ☐   6. _____ ☐

| Done ☑ | Extend ⊘ | Delegate ◉ | Remove ☒ |

20 Minutes ~ Relationship Building
People you introduce your product/service to, new connections and reconnections.

Name	Method of Follow Up/Notes
1. _____	_____
2. _____	_____
3. _____	_____
4. _____	_____
5. _____	_____

20 Minutes ~ Follow Up
Prospects, Clients and Team

Name	Method of Follow Up/Notes
1. _____	_____
2. _____	_____
3. _____	_____
4. _____	_____
5. _____	_____

☐ Instagram   ☐ Birthday Acknowledgement
☐ Facebook   ☐ Recorded Training Audio/Video

Win(s) For The Day:

_____

_____

_____

You are fabulous.

What You Track Grows ...
So Lets Start Tracking

Date: _____

60 Minutes of Daily Focus

20 Minutes ~ Mindset
Gratitude: Today I'm **Grateful** For..

_____

_____

_____

_____

_____

☐ Gratitude - 1 Minute   ☐ Movement - 5 Minutes

☐ Meditation - 2 Minutes   ☐ Read - 10 Minutes

☐ Affirmations - 2 Minutes

Today's 3 Non Negotiables:

_____

_____

_____

To Do:

1. _____ ☐   4. _____ ☐

2. _____ ☐   5. _____ ☐

3. _____ ☐   6. _____ ☐

| Done ☑ | Extend ☑ | Delegate ◉ | Remove ☒ |

20 Minutes ~ Relationship Building
People you introduce your product/service to, new connections and reconnections.

	Name	Method of Follow Up/Notes
1.	_____	_____
2.	_____	_____
3.	_____	_____
4.	_____	_____
5.	_____	_____

20 Minutes ~ Follow Up
Prospects, Clients and Team

	Name	Method of Follow Up/Notes
1.	_____	_____
2.	_____	_____
3.	_____	_____
4.	_____	_____
5.	_____	_____

☐ Instagram
☐ Facebook

☐ Birthday Acknowledgement
☐ Recorded Training Audio/Video

Win(s) For The Day:

_____

_____

_____

You are so smart.

What You Track Grows ...
So Lets Start Tracking

Date: _____

60 Minutes of Daily Focus

20 Minutes ~ Mindset
Gratitude: Today I'm **Grateful** For..

_____
_____
_____
_____
_____

☐ Gratitude - 1 Minute   ☐ Movement - 5 Minutes
☐ Meditation - 2 Minutes   ☐ Read - 10 Minutes
☐ Affirmations - 2 Minutes

Today's 3 Non Negotiables:

_____
_____
_____

To Do:

1. _____ ☐   4. _____ ☐

2. _____ ☐   5. _____ ☐

3. _____ ☐   6. _____ ☐

| Done ☑ | Extend ☑ | Delegate ◎ | Remove ☒ |

20 Minutes ~ Relationship Building
People you introduce your product/service to, new connections and reconnections.

Name   Method of Follow Up/Notes

1. _____   _____

2. _____   _____

3. _____   _____

4. _____   _____

5. _____   _____

20 Minutes ~ Follow Up
Prospects, Clients and Team

Name   Method of Follow Up/Notes

1. _____   _____

2. _____   _____

3. _____   _____

4. _____   _____

5. _____   _____

☐ Instagram   ☐ Birthday Acknowledgement
☐ Facebook   ☐ Recorded Training Audio/Video

Win(s) For The Day:

_____

_____

_____

You make the world a better place.

Notes

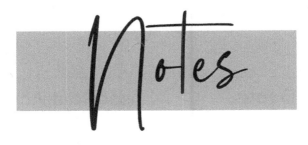

Notes

Monthly Overview

MONTH

This Month's Goals :

Non-Negotiables :

Stretch Goals :

Important Action Steps/ Events

- ○ ....
- ○ ....
- ○ ....
- ○ ....
- ○ ....
- ○ ....
- ○ ....
- ○ ....
- ○ ....
- ○ ....

SU	M	TU	W	TH	F	SA

Notes

"The reason most people never reach their goals is that they don't define them, or ever seriously consider them as believable or achievable. Winners can tell where they are going, what they plan to do along the way, and whp will be sharing the adventure with them."
- Denis Waitley

30 Conversations
in 30 Days

Write down the names of each NEW person you present your product/service to.
This can be in person, a 1-on-1 meeting, at an event or online (including recorded presentations).
Your goal is at least 30 conve sations per month. How close are you?

_____   _____

_____   _____

_____   _____

_____   _____

_____   _____

_____   _____

_____   _____

_____   _____

_____   _____

_____   _____

_____   _____

_____   _____

_____   _____

_____   _____

_____   _____

What You Track Grows ...
So Lets Start Tracking

Date: _____

60 Minutes of Daily Focus

20 Minutes ~ Mindset
Gratitude: Today I'm **Grateful** For..

_____

_____

_____

_____

_____

☐ Gratitude - 1 Minute   ☐ Movement - 5 Minutes

☐ Meditation - 2 Minutes   ☐ Read - 10 Minutes

☐ Affirmations - 2 Minutes

Today's 3 Non Negotiables:

_____

_____

_____

To Do:

1. _____ ☐   4. _____ ☐

2. _____ ☐   5. _____ ☐

3. _____ ☐   6. _____ ☐

| Done ☑ | Extend ☑ | Delegate ◉ | Remove ☒ |

20 Minutes ~ Relationship Building
People you introduce your product/service to, new connections and reconnections.

Name | Method of Follow Up/Notes

1. _____   _____

2. _____   _____

3. _____   _____

4. _____   _____

5. _____   _____

20 Minutes ~ Follow Up
Prospects, Clients and Team

Name | Method of Follow Up/Notes

1. _____   _____

2. _____   _____

3. _____   _____

4. _____   _____

5. _____   _____

☐ Instagram
☐ Facebook

☐ Birthday Acknowledgement
☐ Recorded Training Audio/Video

Win(s) For The Day:

_____

_____

_____

You are one of a kind.

What You Track Grows ...
So Lets Start Tracking

Date: _____

60 Minutes of Daily Focus

20 Minutes ~ Mindset
Gratitude: Today I'm **Grateful** For..

_____

_____

_____

_____

_____

- [ ] Gratitude - 1 Minute
- [ ] Meditation - 2 Minutes
- [ ] Affirmations - 2 Minutes

- [ ] Movement - 5 Minutes
- [ ] Read - 10 Minutes

Today's 3 Non Negotiables:

_____

_____

_____

To Do:

1. _____ [ ]   4. _____ [ ]

2. _____ [ ]   5. _____ [ ]

3. _____ [ ]   6. _____ [ ]

| Done ☑ | Extend ☑ | Delegate ◉ | Remove ☒ |

20 Minutes ~ Relationship Building
People you introduce your product/service to, new connections and reconnections.

Name   Method of Follow Up/Notes

1. _____   _____

2. _____   _____

3. _____   _____

4. _____   _____

5. _____   _____

20 Minutes ~ Follow Up
Prospects, Clients and Team

Name   Method of Follow Up/Notes

1. _____   _____

2. _____   _____

3. _____   _____

4. _____   _____

5. _____   _____

☐ Instagram   ☐ Birthday Acknowledgement
☐ Facebook   ☐ Recorded Training Audio/Video

Win(s) For The Day:

_____

_____

_____

You are radiant.

What You Track Grows ...
So Lets Start Tracking

Date: _____

60 Minutes of Daily Focus

20 Minutes ~ Mindset
Gratitude: Today I'm **Grateful** For..

_____

_____

_____

_____

_____

☐ Gratitude - 1 Minute   ☐ Movement - 5 Minutes

☐ Meditation - 2 Minutes   ☐ Read - 10 Minutes

☐ Affirmations - 2 Minutes

Today's 3 Non Negotiables:

_____

_____

_____

To Do:

1. _____ ☐   4. _____ ☐

2. _____ ☐   5. _____ ☐

3. _____ ☐   6. _____ ☐

| Done ☑ | Extend ⊘ | Delegate ⊙ | Remove ☒ |

20 Minutes ~ Relationship Building

People you introduce your product/service to, new connections and reconnections.

Name   Method of Follow Up/Notes

1. _____   _____

2. _____   _____

3. _____   _____

4. _____   _____

5. _____   _____

20 Minutes ~ Follow Up

Prospects, Clients and Team

Name   Method of Follow Up/Notes

1. _____   _____

2. _____   _____

3. _____   _____

4. _____   _____

5. _____   _____

☐ Instagram   ☐ Birthday Acknowledgement
☐ Facebook   ☐ Recorded Training Audio/Video

Win(s) For The Day:

_____

_____

_____

You are braver than you think.

What You Track Grows ...
So Lets Start Tracking

Date: _____

60 Minutes of Daily Focus

20 Minutes ~ Mindset
Gratitude: Today I'm **Grateful** For..

_____   _____

_____   _____

_____   _____

_____   _____

☐ Gratitude - 1 Minute   ☐ Movement - 5 Minutes
☐ Meditation - 2 Minutes   ☐ Read - 10 Minutes
☐ Affirmations - 2 Minutes

Today's 3 Non Negotiables:

_____   _____

_____   _____

_____   _____

To Do:

1. _____ ☐   4. _____ ☐

2. _____ ☐   5. _____ ☐

3. _____ ☐   6. _____ ☐

| Done ☑ | Extend ☑ | Delegate ◨ | Remove ☒ |

20 Minutes ~ Relationship Building
People you introduce your product/service to, new connections and reconnections.

Name   Method of Follow Up/Notes

1. _____   _____

2. _____   _____

3. _____   _____

4. _____   _____

5. _____   _____

20 Minutes ~ Follow Up
Prospects, Clients and Team

Name   Method of Follow Up/Notes

1. _____   _____

2. _____   _____

3. _____   _____

4. _____   _____

5. _____   _____

☐ Instagram   ☐ Birthday Acknowledgement
☐ Facebook   ☐ Recorded Training Audio/Video

Win(s) For The Day:

_____

_____

_____

You are such a blessing.

What You Track Grows ...
So Lets Start Tracking

Date: _____

60 Minutes of Daily Focus

20 Minutes ~ Mindset
Gratitude: Today I'm **Grateful** For..

_____

_____

_____

_____

_____

- ☐ Gratitude - 1 Minute
- ☐ Meditation - 2 Minutes
- ☐ Affirmations - 2 Minutes

- ☐ Movement - 5 Minutes
- ☐ Read - 10 Minutes

Today's 3 Non Negotiables:

_____

_____

_____

To Do:

1. _____ ☐   4. _____ ☐

2. _____ ☐   5. _____ ☐

3. _____ ☐   6. _____ ☐

| Done ☑ | Extend ☑ | Delegate ◉ | Remove ☒ |

20 Minutes ~ Relationship Building

People you introduce your product/service to, new connections and reconnections.

Name	Method of Follow Up/Notes
1. _____	_____
2. _____	_____
3. _____	_____
4. _____	_____
5. _____	_____

20 Minutes ~ Follow Up

Prospects, Clients and Team

Name	Method of Follow Up/Notes
1. _____	_____
2. _____	_____
3. _____	_____
4. _____	_____
5. _____	_____

☐ Instagram
☐ Facebook

☐ Birthday Acknowledgement
☐ Recorded Training Audio/Video

Win(s) For The Day:

_____

_____

_____

You are powerful.

What You Track Grows ...
So Lets Start Tracking

Date: _____

60 Minutes of Daily Focus

20 Minutes ~ Mindset
Gratitude: Today I'm **Grateful** For..

_____

_____

_____

_____

_____

- ☐ Gratitude - 1 Minute
- ☐ Meditation - 2 Minutes
- ☐ Affirmations - 2 Minutes

- ☐ Movement - 5 Minutes
- ☐ Read - 10 Minutes

Today's 3 Non Negotiables:

_____

_____

_____

To Do:

1. _____ ☐
2. _____ ☐
3. _____ ☐

4. _____ ☐
5. _____ ☐
6. _____ ☐

| Done ☑ | Extend ⧄ | Delegate ⊚ | Remove ☒ |

20 Minutes ~ Relationship Building
People you introduce your product/service to, new connections and reconnections.

Name

1. _____
2. _____
3. _____
4. _____
5. _____

Method of Follow Up/Notes

_____

_____

_____

_____

_____

20 Minutes ~ Follow Up
Prospects, Clients and Team

Name

1. _____
2. _____
3. _____
4. _____
5. _____

Method of Follow Up/Notes

_____

_____

_____

_____

_____

☐ Instagram
☐ Facebook

☐ Birthday Acknowledgement
☐ Recorded Training Audio/Video

Win(s) For The Day:

_____

_____

_____

Your smile is contagious.

What You Track Grows ...
So Lets Start Tracking

Date: _____

60 Minutes of Daily Focus

20 Minutes ~ Mindset
Gratitude: Today I'm **Grateful** For..

_____

_____

_____

_____

_____

☐ Gratitude - 1 Minute   ☐ Movement - 5 Minutes

☐ Meditation - 2 Minutes   ☐ Read - 10 Minutes

☐ Affirmations - 2 Minutes

Today's 3 Non Negotiables:

_____

_____

_____

To Do:

1. _____ ☐   4. _____ ☐

2. _____ ☐   5. _____ ☐

3. _____ ☐   6. _____ ☐

| Done ☑ | Extend ☑ | Delegate ◉ | Remove ☒ |

20 Minutes ~ Relationship Building
People you introduce your product/service to, new connections and reconnections.

Name	Method of Follow Up/Notes
1. _____	_____
2. _____	_____
3. _____	_____
4. _____	_____
5. _____	_____

20 Minutes ~ Follow Up
Prospects, Clients and Team

Name	Method of Follow Up/Notes
1. _____	_____
2. _____	_____
3. _____	_____
4. _____	_____
5. _____	_____

☐ Instagram   ☐ Birthday Acknowledgement
☐ Facebook   ☐ Recorded Training Audio/Video

Win(s) For The Day:

_____

_____

_____

You make the world a better place.

What You Track Grows ...
So Lets Start Tracking

Date: _____

60 Minutes of Daily Focus

20 Minutes ~ Mindset
Gratitude: Today I'm **Grateful** For..

_____

_____

_____

_____

☐ Gratitude - 1 Minute   ☐ Movement - 5 Minutes

☐ Meditation - 2 Minutes   ☐ Read - 10 Minutes

☐ Affirmations - 2 Minutes

Today's 3 Non Negotiables:

_____

_____

_____

To Do:

1. _____ ☐   4. _____ ☐

2. _____ ☐   5. _____ ☐

3. _____ ☐   6. _____ ☐

| Done ☑ | Extend ☑ | Delegate ◉ | Remove ☒ |

20 Minutes ~ Relationship Building
People you introduce your product/service to, new connections and reconnections.

Name	Method of Follow Up/Notes
1. _____	_____
2. _____	_____
3. _____	_____
4. _____	_____
5. _____	_____

20 Minutes ~ Follow Up
Prospects, Clients and Team

Name	Method of Follow Up/Notes
1. _____	_____
2. _____	_____
3. _____	_____
4. _____	_____
5. _____	_____

☐ Instagram
☐ Facebook

☐ Birthday Acknowledgement
☐ Recorded Training Audio/Video

Win(s) For The Day:

_____

_____

_____

You have the best ideas.

What You Track Grows ...
So Lets Start Tracking

Date: _____

60 Minutes of Daily Focus

20 Minutes ~ Mindset
Gratitude: Today I'm **Grateful** For..

_____

_____

_____

_____

_____

☐ Gratitude - 1 Minute   ☐ Movement - 5 Minutes

☐ Meditation - 2 Minutes   ☐ Read - 10 Minutes

☐ Affirmations - 2 Minutes

Today's 3 Non Negotiables:

_____

_____

_____

To Do:

1. _____ ☐   4. _____ ☐

2. _____ ☐   5. _____ ☐

3. _____ ☐   6. _____ ☐

| Done ☑ | Extend ⧄ | Delegate ⊡ | Remove ☒ |

20 Minutes ~ Relationship Building

People you introduce your product/service to, new connections and reconnections.

Name   Method of Follow Up/Notes

1. _____   _____

2. _____   _____

3. _____   _____

4. _____   _____

5. _____   _____

20 Minutes ~ Follow Up

Prospects, Clients and Team

Name   Method of Follow Up/Notes

1. _____   _____

2. _____   _____

3. _____   _____

4. _____   _____

5. _____   _____

☐ Instagram   ☐ Birthday Acknowledgement
☐ Facebook   ☐ Recorded Training Audio/Video

Win(s) For The Day:

_____

_____

_____

You are perfect just the way you are.

What You Track Grows ...

So Lets Start Tracking

Date: _____

60 Minutes of Daily Focus

20 Minutes ~ Mindset
Gratitude: Today I'm **Grateful** For..

_____ _____

_____ _____

_____ _____

_____ _____

_____ _____

☐ Gratitude - 1 Minute   ☐ Movement - 5 Minutes

☐ Meditation - 2 Minutes   ☐ Read - 10 Minutes

☐ Affirmations - 2 Minutes

Today's 3 Non Negotiables:

_____ _____

_____ _____

_____ _____

To Do:

1. _____ ☐   4. _____ ☐

2. _____ ☐   5. _____ ☐

3. _____ ☐   6. _____ ☐

| Done ☑ | Extend ☑ | Delegate ◎ | Remove ☒ |

20 Minutes ~ Relationship Building
People you introduce your product/service to, new connections and reconnections.

Name	Method of Follow Up/Notes
1. _____	_____
2. _____	_____
3. _____	_____
4. _____	_____
5. _____	_____

20 Minutes ~ Follow Up
Prospects, Clients and Team

Name	Method of Follow Up/Notes
1. _____	_____
2. _____	_____
3. _____	_____
4. _____	_____
5. _____	_____

☐ Instagram
☐ Facebook

☐ Birthday Acknowledgement
☐ Recorded Training Audio/Video

Win(s) For The Day:

_____

_____

_____

You are magic.

What You Track Grows ...
So Lets Start Tracking

Date: _____

60 Minutes of Daily Focus

20 Minutes ~ Mindset
Gratitude: Today I'm **Grateful** For..

_____

_____

_____

_____

_____

☐ Gratitude - 1 Minute   ☐ Movement - 5 Minutes

☐ Meditation - 2 Minutes   ☐ Read - 10 Minutes

☐ Affirmations - 2 Minutes

Today's 3 Non Negotiables:

_____

_____

_____

To Do:

1. _____ ☐   4. _____ ☐

2. _____ ☐   5. _____ ☐

3. _____ ☐   6. _____ ☐

Done ☑   **Extend** ☑   **Delegate** ◎   **Remove** ☒

20 Minutes ~ Relationship Building
People you introduce your product/service to, new connections and reconnections.

Name	Method of Follow Up/Notes
1. _____	_____
2. _____	_____
3. _____	_____
4. _____	_____
5. _____	_____

20 Minutes ~ Follow Up
Prospects, Clients and Team

Name	Method of Follow Up/Notes
1. _____	_____
2. _____	_____
3. _____	_____
4. _____	_____
5. _____	_____

☐ Instagram
☐ Facebook

☐ Birthday Acknowledgement
☐ Recorded Training Audio/Video

Win(s) For The Day:

_____

_____

_____

You are inspiring.

What You Track Grows ...
So Lets Start Tracking

Date: _____

60 Minutes of Daily Focus

20 Minutes ~ Mindset
Gratitude: Today I'm **Grateful** For..

_____

_____

_____

_____

_____

☐ Gratitude - 1 Minute   ☐ Movement - 5 Minutes
☐ Meditation - 2 Minutes   ☐ Read - 10 Minutes
☐ Affirmations - 2 Minutes

Today's 3 Non Negotiables:

_____

_____

_____

To Do:

1. _____ ☐   4. _____ ☐

2. _____ ☐   5. _____ ☐

3. _____ ☐   6. _____ ☐

| Done ☑ | Extend ☑ | Delegate ◎ | Remove ☒ |

20 Minutes ~ Relationship Building
People you introduce your product/service to, new connections and reconnections.

Name | Method of Follow Up/Notes

1. _____   _____

2. _____   _____

3. _____   _____

4. _____   _____

5. _____   _____

20 Minutes ~ Follow Up
Prospects, Clients and Team

Name | Method of Follow Up/Notes

1. _____   _____

2. _____   _____

3. _____   _____

4. _____   _____

5. _____   _____

☐ Instagram   ☐ Birthday Acknowledgement
☐ Facebook   ☐ Recorded Training Audio/Video

Win(s) For The Day:

_____

_____

_____

You are so worthy of a beautiful life.

What You Track Grows ...
So Lets Start Tracking

Date: _____

60 Minutes of Daily Focus

20 Minutes ~ Mindset
Gratitude: Today I'm **Grateful** For..

_____

_____

_____

_____

_____

☐ Gratitude - 1 Minute   ☐ Movement - 5 Minutes

☐ Meditation - 2 Minutes   ☐ Read - 10 Minutes

☐ Affirmations - 2 Minutes

Today's 3 Non Negotiables:

_____

_____

_____

To Do:

1. _____ ☐   4. _____ ☐

2. _____ ☐   5. _____ ☐

3. _____ ☐   6. _____ ☐

| Done ☑ | Extend ☑ | Delegate ◙ | Remove ☒ |

20 Minutes ~ Relationship Building
People you introduce your product/service to, new connections and reconnections.

Name   Method of Follow Up/Notes

1. _____   _____

2. _____   _____

3. _____   _____

4. _____   _____

5. _____   _____

20 Minutes ~ Follow Up
Prospects, Clients and Team

Name   Method of Follow Up/Notes

1. _____   _____

2. _____   _____

3. _____   _____

4. _____   _____

5. _____   _____

☐ Instagram   ☐ Birthday Acknowledgement
☐ Facebook   ☐ Recorded Training Audio/Video

Win(s) For The Day:

_____

_____

_____

You've totally got this.

What You Track Grows ...
So Lets Start Tracking

Date: _____

60 Minutes of Daily Focus

20 Minutes ~ Mindset
Gratitude: Today I'm **Grateful** For..

_____

_____

_____

_____

_____

☐ Gratitude - 1 Minute   ☐ Movement - 5 Minutes

☐ Meditation - 2 Minutes   ☐ Read - 10 Minutes

☐ Affirmations - 2 Minutes

Today's 3 Non Negotiables:

_____

_____

_____

To Do:

1. _____ ☐   4. _____ ☐

2. _____ ☐   5. _____ ☐

3. _____ ☐   6. _____ ☐

| Done ☑ | Extend ☑ | Delegate ◉ | Remove ☒ |

20 Minutes ~ Relationship Building

People you introduce your product/service to, new connections and reconnections.

Name | Method of Follow Up/Notes

1. _____   _____

2. _____   _____

3. _____   _____

4. _____   _____

5. _____   _____

20 Minutes ~ Follow Up

Prospects, Clients and Team

Name | Method of Follow Up/Notes

1. _____   _____

2. _____   _____

3. _____   _____

4. _____   _____

5. _____   _____

☐ Instagram   ☐ Birthday Acknowledgement
☐ Facebook   ☐ Recorded Training Audio/Video

Win(s) For The Day:

_____

_____

_____

You define kind.

What You Track Grows ...
So Lets Start Tracking

Date: _____

60 Minutes of Daily Focus

20 Minutes ~ Mindset
Gratitude: Today I'm **Grateful** For..

_____

_____

_____

_____

_____

☐ Gratitude - 1 Minute   ☐ Movement - 5 Minutes
☐ Meditation - 2 Minutes   ☐ Read - 10 Minutes
☐ Affirmations - 2 Minutes

Today's 3 Non Negotiables:

_____

_____

_____

To Do:

1. _____ ☐   4. _____ ☐

2. _____ ☐   5. _____ ☐

3. _____ ☐   6. _____ ☐

| Done ☑ | Extend ☑ | Delegate ☑ | Remove ☒ |

20 Minutes ~ Relationship Building
People you introduce your product/service to, new connections and reconnections.

	Name	Method of Follow Up/Notes
1.	_____	_____
2.	_____	_____
3.	_____	_____
4.	_____	_____
5.	_____	_____

20 Minutes ~ Follow Up
Prospects, Clients and Team

	Name	Method of Follow Up/Notes
1.	_____	_____
2.	_____	_____
3.	_____	_____
4.	_____	_____
5.	_____	_____

☐ Instagram
☐ Facebook

☐ Birthday Acknowledgement
☐ Recorded Training Audio/Video

Win(s) For The Day:

_____

_____

_____

You are a rockstar.

What You Track Grows ...
So Lets Start Tracking

Date: _____

60 Minutes of Daily Focus

20 Minutes ~ Mindset
Gratitude: Today I'm **Grateful** For..

_____

_____

_____

_____

- ☐ Gratitude - 1 Minute
- ☐ Meditation - 2 Minutes
- ☐ Affirmations - 2 Minutes

- ☐ Movement - 5 Minutes
- ☐ Read - 10 Minutes

Today's 3 Non Negotiables:

_____

_____

_____

To Do:

1. _____ ☐   4. _____ ☐

2. _____ ☐   5. _____ ☐

3. _____ ☐   6. _____ ☐

| Done ☑ | Extend ☑ | Delegate ◎ | Remove ☒ |

20 Minutes ~ Relationship Building
People you introduce your product/service to, new connections and reconnections.

Name   Method of Follow Up/Notes

1. _____   _____

2. _____   _____

3. _____   _____

4. _____   _____

5. _____   _____

20 Minutes ~ Follow Up
Prospects, Clients and Team

Name   Method of Follow Up/Notes

1. _____   _____

2. _____   _____

3. _____   _____

4. _____   _____

5. _____   _____

☐ Instagram   ☐ Birthday Acknowledgement
☐ Facebook   ☐ Recorded Training Audio/Video

Win(s) For The Day:

_____

_____

_____

More people should be like you.

What You Track Grows ...
So Lets Start Tracking

Date: _____

60 Minutes of Daily Focus

20 Minutes ~ Mindset
Gratitude: Today I'm **Grateful** For..

_____

_____

_____

_____

_____

☐ Gratitude - 1 Minute   ☐ Movement - 5 Minutes
☐ Meditation - 2 Minutes   ☐ Read - 10 Minutes
☐ Affirmations - 2 Minutes

Today's 3 Non Negotiables:

_____

_____

_____

To Do:

1. _____ ☐   4. _____ ☐

2. _____ ☐   5. _____ ☐

3. _____ ☐   6. _____ ☐

Done ☑   Extend ☑   Delegate ◎   Remove ☒

20 Minutes ~ Relationship Building
People you introduce your product/service to, new connections and reconnections.

Name	Method of Follow Up/Notes
1. _____	_____
2. _____	_____
3. _____	_____
4. _____	_____
5. _____	_____

20 Minutes ~ Follow Up
Prospects, Clients and Team

Name	Method of Follow Up/Notes
1. _____	_____
2. _____	_____
3. _____	_____
4. _____	_____
5. _____	_____

☐ Instagram
☐ Facebook

☐ Birthday Acknowledgement
☐ Recorded Training Audio/Video

Win(s) For The Day:

_____

_____

_____

You're doing a great job.

What You Track Grows ...
So Lets Start Tracking

Date: _____

60 Minutes of Daily Focus

20 Minutes ~ Mindset
Gratitude: Today I'm **Grateful** For..

_____

_____

_____

_____

☐ Gratitude - 1 Minute   ☐ Movement - 5 Minutes

☐ Meditation - 2 Minutes   ☐ Read - 10 Minutes

☐ Affirmations - 2 Minutes

Today's 3 Non Negotiables:

_____

_____

_____

To Do:

1. _____ ☐   4. _____ ☐

2. _____ ☐   5. _____ ☐

3. _____ ☐   6. _____ ☐

| Done ☑ | Extend ☑ | Delegate ⊡ | Remove ☒ |

20 Minutes ~ Relationship Building
People you introduce your product/service to, new connections and reconnections.

Name   Method of Follow Up/Notes

1. _____   _____

2. _____   _____

3. _____   _____

4. _____   _____

5. _____   _____

20 Minutes ~ Follow Up
Prospects, Clients and Team

Name   Method of Follow Up/Notes

1. _____   _____

2. _____   _____

3. _____   _____

4. _____   _____

5. _____   _____

☐ Instagram   ☐ Birthday Acknowledgement
☐ Facebook   ☐ Recorded Training Audio/Video

Win(s) For The Day:

_____

_____

_____

You are enough.

What You Track Grows ...

So Lets Start Tracking

Date: _____

60 Minutes of Daily Focus

20 Minutes ~ Mindset
Gratitude: Today I'm **Grateful** For..

_____

_____

_____

_____

_____

- ☐ Gratitude - 1 Minute
- ☐ Meditation - 2 Minutes
- ☐ Affirmations - 2 Minutes

- ☐ Movement - 5 Minutes
- ☐ Read - 10 Minutes

Today's 3 Non Negotiables:

_____

_____

_____

To Do:

1. _____ ☐   4. _____ ☐

2. _____ ☐   5. _____ ☐

3. _____ ☐   6. _____ ☐

| Done ☑ | Extend ☑ | Delegate ◉ | Remove ☒ |

20 Minutes ~ Relationship Building
People you introduce your product/service to, new connections and reconnections.

	Name	Method of Follow Up/Notes
1.	_____	_____
2.	_____	_____
3.	_____	_____
4.	_____	_____
5.	_____	_____

20 Minutes ~ Follow Up
Prospects, Clients and Team

	Name	Method of Follow Up/Notes
1.	_____	_____
2.	_____	_____
3.	_____	_____
4.	_____	_____
5.	_____	_____

☐ Instagram
☐ Facebook

☐ Birthday Acknowledgement
☐ Recorded Training Audio/Video

Win(s) For The Day:

_____

_____

_____

You always go above and beyond.

What You Track Grows ...
So Lets Start Tracking

Date: _____

60 Minutes of Daily Focus

20 Minutes ~ Mindset
Gratitude: Today I'm **Grateful** For..

_____

_____

_____

_____

_____

☐ Gratitude - 1 Minute   ☐ Movement - 5 Minutes

☐ Meditation - 2 Minutes   ☐ Read - 10 Minutes

☐ Affirmations - 2 Minutes

Today's 3 Non Negotiables:

_____

_____

_____

To Do:

1. _____ ☐   4. _____ ☐

2. _____ ☐   5. _____ ☐

3. _____ ☐   6. _____ ☐

| Done ☑ | Extend ☑ | Delegate ⊡ | Remove ☒ |

20 Minutes ~ Relationship Building
People you introduce your product/service to, new connections and reconnections.

	Name	Method of Follow Up/Notes
1.	_____	_____
2.	_____	_____
3.	_____	_____
4.	_____	_____
5.	_____	_____

20 Minutes ~ Follow Up
Prospects, Clients and Team

	Name	Method of Follow Up/Notes
1.	_____	_____
2.	_____	_____
3.	_____	_____
4.	_____	_____
5.	_____	_____

☐ Instagram
☐ Facebook

☐ Birthday Acknowledgement
☐ Recorded Training Audio/Video

Win(s) For The Day:

_____

_____

_____

You are capable of amazing things.

What You Track Grows ...
So Lets Start Tracking

Date: _____

60 Minutes of Daily Focus

20 Minutes ~ Mindset
Gratitude: Today I'm **Grateful** For..

_____

_____

_____

_____

_____

☐ Gratitude - 1 Minute   ☐ Movement - 5 Minutes

☐ Meditation - 2 Minutes   ☐ Read - 10 Minutes

☐ Affirmations - 2 Minutes

Today's 3 Non Negotiables:

_____

_____

_____

To Do:

1. _____ ☐   4. _____ ☐

2. _____ ☐   5. _____ ☐

3. _____ ☐   6. _____ ☐

| Done ☑ | Extend ⧄ | Delegate ◉ | Remove ☒ |

20 Minutes ~ Relationship Building
People you introduce your product/service to, new connections and reconnections.

	Name	Method of Follow Up/Notes
1.	_____	_____
2.	_____	_____
3.	_____	_____
4.	_____	_____
5.	_____	_____

20 Minutes ~ Follow Up
Prospects, Clients and Team

	Name	Method of Follow Up/Notes
1.	_____	_____
2.	_____	_____
3.	_____	_____
4.	_____	_____
5.	_____	_____

☐ Instagram
☐ Facebook

☐ Birthday Acknowledgement
☐ Recorded Training Audio/Video

Win(s) For The Day:

_____

_____

_____

You are capable of amazing things.

What You Track Grows ...
So Lets Start Tracking

Date: _____

60 Minutes of Daily Focus

20 Minutes ~ Mindset
Gratitude: Today I'm **Grateful** For..

_____

_____

_____

_____

_____

☐ Gratitude - 1 Minute   ☐ Movement - 5 Minutes
☐ Meditation - 2 Minutes   ☐ Read - 10 Minutes
☐ Affirmations - 2 Minutes

Today's 3 Non Negotiables:

_____

_____

_____

To Do:

1. _____ ☐   4. _____ ☐

2. _____ ☐   5. _____ ☐

3. _____ ☐   6. _____ ☐

| Done ☑ | Extend ☐ | Delegate ◎ | Remove ☒ |

20 Minutes ~ Relationship Building
People you introduce your product/service to, new connections and reconnections.

Name   Method of Follow Up/Notes

1. _____   _____

2. _____   _____

3. _____   _____

4. _____   _____

5. _____   _____

20 Minutes ~ Follow Up
Prospects, Clients and Team

Name   Method of Follow Up/Notes

1. _____   _____

2. _____   _____

3. _____   _____

4. _____   _____

5. _____   _____

☐ Instagram   ☐ Birthday Acknowledgement
☐ Facebook   ☐ Recorded Training Audio/Video

Win(s) For The Day:

_____

_____

_____

You are so loved.

What You Track Grows ...

So Lets Start Tracking

Date: _____

60 Minutes of Daily Focus

20 Minutes ~ Mindset
Gratitude: Today I'm **Grateful** For..

_____

_____

_____

_____

_____

☐ Gratitude - 1 Minute   ☐ Movement - 5 Minutes

☐ Meditation - 2 Minutes   ☐ Read - 10 Minutes

☐ Affirmations - 2 Minutes

Today's 3 Non Negotiables:

_____

_____

_____

To Do:

1. _____ ☐   4. _____ ☐

2. _____ ☐   5. _____ ☐

3. _____ ☐   6. _____ ☐

| Done ☑ | Extend ☑ | Delegate ◙ | Remove ☒ |

20 Minutes ~ Relationship Building
People you introduce your product/service to, new connections and reconnections.

Name	Method of Follow Up/Notes
1. _____	_____
2. _____	_____
3. _____	_____
4. _____	_____
5. _____	_____

20 Minutes ~ Follow Up
Prospects, Clients and Team

Name	Method of Follow Up/Notes
1. _____	_____
2. _____	_____
3. _____	_____
4. _____	_____
5. _____	_____

☐ Instagram
☐ Facebook

☐ Birthday Acknowledgement
☐ Recorded Training Audio/Video

Win(s) For The Day:

_____

_____

_____

Be kind to yourself.

What You Track Grows ...
So Lets Start Tracking

Date: _____

60 Minutes of Daily Focus

20 Minutes ~ Mindset
Gratitude: Today I'm **Grateful** For..

_____

_____

_____

_____

_____

☐ Gratitude - 1 Minute   ☐ Movement - 5 Minutes

☐ Meditation - 2 Minutes   ☐ Read - 10 Minutes

☐ Affirmations - 2 Minutes

Today's 3 Non Negotiables:

_____

_____

_____

To Do:

1. _____ ☐   4. _____ ☐

2. _____ ☐   5. _____ ☐

3. _____ ☐   6. _____ ☐

| Done ☑ | Extend ☑ | Delegate ◉ | Remove ☒ |

20 Minutes ~ Relationship Building
People you introduce your product/service to, new connections and reconnections.

Name | Method of Follow Up/Notes

1. _____ _____

2. _____ _____

3. _____ _____

4. _____ _____

5. _____ _____

20 Minutes ~ Follow Up
Prospects, Clients and Team

Name | Method of Follow Up/Notes

1. _____ _____

2. _____ _____

3. _____ _____

4. _____ _____

5. _____ _____

☐ Instagram
☐ Facebook

☐ Birthday Acknowledgement
☐ Recorded Training Audio/Video

Win(s) For The Day:

_____

_____

_____

Never forget how beautiful you are.

What You Track Grows ...
So Lets Start Tracking

Date: _____

60 Minutes of Daily Focus

20 Minutes ~ Mindset
Gratitude: Today I'm **Grateful** For..

_____

_____

_____

_____

_____

☐ Gratitude - 1 Minute   ☐ Movement - 5 Minutes
☐ Meditation - 2 Minutes   ☐ Read - 10 Minutes
☐ Affirmations - 2 Minutes

Today's 3 Non Negotiables:

_____

_____

_____

To Do:

1. _____ ☐   4. _____ ☐

2. _____ ☐   5. _____ ☐

3. _____ ☐   6. _____ ☐

| Done ☑ | Extend ☑ | Delegate ◎ | Remove ☒ |

20 Minutes ~ Relationship Building

People you introduce your product/service to, new connections and reconnections.

Name   Method of Follow Up/Notes

1. _____   _____

2. _____   _____

3. _____   _____

4. _____   _____

5. _____   _____

20 Minutes ~ Follow Up

Prospects, Clients and Team

Name   Method of Follow Up/Notes

1. _____   _____

2. _____   _____

3. _____   _____

4. _____   _____

5. _____   _____

☐ Instagram   ☐ Birthday Acknowledgement
☐ Facebook   ☐ Recorded Training Audio/Video

Win(s) For The Day:

_____

_____

_____

You look especially lovely today.

Date: _____

60 Minutes of Daily Focus

20 Minutes ~ Mindset
Gratitude: Today I'm **Grateful** For..

_____

_____

_____

_____

_____

☐ Gratitude - 1 Minute   ☐ Movement - 5 Minutes

☐ Meditation - 2 Minutes   ☐ Read - 10 Minutes

☐ Affirmations - 2 Minutes

Today's 3 Non Negotiables:

_____

_____

_____

To Do:

1. _____ ☐   4. _____ ☐

2. _____ ☐   5. _____ ☐

3. _____ ☐   6. _____ ☐

| Done ☑ | Extend ☑ | Delegate ◎ | Remove ☒ |

20 Minutes ~ Relationship Building
People you introduce your product/service to, new connections and reconnections.

	Name	Method of Follow Up/Notes
1.	_____	_____
2.	_____	_____
3.	_____	_____
4.	_____	_____
5.	_____	_____

20 Minutes ~ Follow Up
Prospects, Clients and Team

	Name	Method of Follow Up/Notes
1.	_____	_____
2.	_____	_____
3.	_____	_____
4.	_____	_____
5.	_____	_____

☐ Instagram
☐ Facebook

☐ Birthday Acknowledgement
☐ Recorded Training Audio/Video

Win(s) For The Day:

_____

_____

_____

Thanks for being you   .

What You Track Grows ...
So Lets Start Tracking

Date: _____

60 Minutes of Daily Focus

20 Minutes ~ Mindset
Gratitude: Today I'm ***Grateful*** For..

_____

_____

_____

_____

_____

☐ Gratitude - 1 Minute   ☐ Movement - 5 Minutes

☐ Meditation - 2 Minutes   ☐ Read - 10 Minutes

☐ Affirmations - 2 Minutes

Today's 3 Non Negotiables:

_____

_____

_____

To Do:

1. _____ ☐   4. _____ ☐

2. _____ ☐   5. _____ ☐

3. _____ ☐   6. _____ ☐

| Done ☑ | Extend ☑ | Delegate ◎ | Remove ☒ |

20 Minutes ~ Relationship Building
People you introduce your product/service to, new connections and reconnections.

Name	Method of Follow Up/Notes
1. _____	_____
2. _____	_____
3. _____	_____
4. _____	_____
5. _____	_____

20 Minutes ~ Follow Up
Prospects, Clients and Team

Name	Method of Follow Up/Notes
1. _____	_____
2. _____	_____
3. _____	_____
4. _____	_____
5. _____	_____

☐ Instagram
☐ Facebook

☐ Birthday Acknowledgement
☐ Recorded Training Audio/Video

Win(s) For The Day:

_____

_____

_____

Your possibilities are endless.

What You Track Grows ...
So Lets Start Tracking

Date: _____

60 Minutes of Daily Focus

20 Minutes ~ Mindset
Gratitude: Today I'm **Grateful** For..

_____
_____
_____
_____
_____

- ☐ Gratitude - 1 Minute
- ☐ Meditation - 2 Minutes
- ☐ Affirmations - 2 Minutes

- ☐ Movement - 5 Minutes
- ☐ Read - 10 Minutes

Today's 3 Non Negotiables:

_____
_____
_____

To Do:

1. _____ ☐
2. _____ ☐
3. _____ ☐

4. _____ ☐
5. _____ ☐
6. _____ ☐

Done ☑   Extend ☑   Delegate ☑   Remove ☒

20 Minutes ~ Relationship Building
People you introduce your product/service to, new connections and reconnections.

Name | Method of Follow Up/Notes

1. _____ | _____

2. _____ | _____

3. _____ | _____

4. _____ | _____

5. _____ | _____

20 Minutes ~ Follow Up
Prospects, Clients and Team

Name | Method of Follow Up/Notes

1. _____ | _____

2. _____ | _____

3. _____ | _____

4. _____ | _____

5. _____ | _____

☐ Instagram   ☐ Birthday Acknowledgement
☐ Facebook   ☐ Recorded Training Audio/Video

Win(s) For The Day:

_____

_____

_____

You are fabulous.

What You Track Grows ...
So Lets Start Tracking

Date: _____

60 Minutes of Daily Focus

20 Minutes ~ Mindset
Gratitude: Today I'm **Grateful** For..

_____

_____

_____

_____

_____

☐ Gratitude - 1 Minute   ☐ Movement - 5 Minutes

☐ Meditation - 2 Minutes   ☐ Read - 10 Minutes

☐ Affirmations - 2 Minutes

Today's 3 Non Negotiables:

_____

_____

_____

To Do:

1. _____ ☐   4. _____ ☐

2. _____ ☐   5. _____ ☐

3. _____ ☐   6. _____ ☐

| Done ☑ | Extend ⊡ | Delegate ⊙ | Remove ☒ |

20 Minutes ~ Relationship Building
People you introduce your product/service to, new connections and reconnections.

Name	Method of Follow Up/Notes
1. _____	_____
2. _____	_____
3. _____	_____
4. _____	_____
5. _____	_____

20 Minutes ~ Follow Up
Prospects, Clients and Team

Name	Method of Follow Up/Notes
1. _____	_____
2. _____	_____
3. _____	_____
4. _____	_____
5. _____	_____

☐ Instagram   ☐ Birthday Acknowledgement
☐ Facebook   ☐ Recorded Training Audio/Video

Win(s) For The Day:

_____

_____

_____

You are so smart.

What You Track Grows ...
So Lets Start Tracking

Date: _____

60 Minutes of Daily Focus

20 Minutes ~ Mindset
Gratitude: Today I'm **Grateful** For..

_____

_____

_____

_____

_____

☐ Gratitude - 1 Minute   ☐ Movement - 5 Minutes

☐ Meditation - 2 Minutes   ☐ Read - 10 Minutes

☐ Affirmations - 2 Minutes

Today's 3 Non Negotiables:

_____

_____

_____

To Do:

1. _____ ☐   4. _____ ☐

2. _____ ☐   5. _____ ☐

3. _____ ☐   6. _____ ☐

| Done ☑ | Extend ☑ | Delegate ☑ | Remove ☒ |

20 Minutes ~ Relationship Building
People you introduce your product/service to, new connections and reconnections.

Name	Method of Follow Up/Notes
1. _____	_____
2. _____	_____
3. _____	_____
4. _____	_____
5. _____	_____

20 Minutes ~ Follow Up
Prospects, Clients and Team

Name	Method of Follow Up/Notes
1. _____	_____
2. _____	_____
3. _____	_____
4. _____	_____
5. _____	_____

☐ Instagram
☐ Facebook

☐ Birthday Acknowledgement
☐ Recorded Training Audio/Video

Win(s) For The Day:

_____

_____

_____

You make the world a better place.

Notes

Notes

Notes